● ● ● ● ● ● ● ● ● ● ● ● ● ● ●

A Guide to Field Research

THE PINE FORGE PRESS SERIES IN RESEARCH METHODS AND STATISTICS

Richard T. Campbell and Kathleen S. Crittenden, Series Editors

Through its unique modular format, this series offers an unmatched flexibility and coherence for undergraduate methods and statistics teaching. The two "core" volumes, one in methods and one in statistics, address the primary concerns of undergraduate courses, but in less detail than found in existing texts, and are both available in inexpensive, paperback editions. The smaller "satellite" volumes in the series can either supplement these core books, giving instructors the emphasis and coverage best suited for their course and students, or be used in more advanced, specialized courses.

Investigating the Social World:
The Process and Practice of Research *by Russell K. Schutt*

A Guide to Field Research *by Carol A. Bailey*

Designing Surveys: A Guide to Decisions and Procedures *by Ronald Czaja and Johnny Blair*

How Sampling Works *by Richard Maisel and Caroline Hodges Persell*

Forthcoming

Introduction to Social Statistics *by Chava Frankfort-Nachmias*

Regression: A Primer *by Richard T. Campbell and Kathleen S. Crittenden*

Experimental Design and Analysis of Variance *by Robert Leik*

Analyzing Data *by James Davis and Jere Bruner*

Applied Social Research *by Marty Jendrek*

● ● ● ● ● ● ● ● ● ● ● ● ●

A Guide to Field Research

Carol A. Bailey
Virginia Polytechnic Institute and State University

Pine Forge Press

Thousand Oaks, California • London • New Delhi

For information, address:

 Pine Forge Press
A Sage Publications Company
2455 Teller Road
Thousand Oaks, California 91320
(805) 499-4224
E-mail: sales@pfp.sagepub.com

SAGE Publications Ltd.
6 Bonhill Street
London EC2A 4PU
United Kingdom

SAGE Publications India Pvt. Ltd.
M-32 Market
Greater Kailash I
New Delhi, 110 048 India

Production and Typesetting: Scratchgravel Publishing Services
Production Manager: Rebecca Holland
Designer: Lisa S. Mirski
Cover Design: Paula Shuhert and Graham Metcalfe

Printed in the United States of America

98 99 10 9 8 7 6 5 4 3

Library of Congress Cataloging-in-Publication Data
Bailey, Carol A., 1950–
    A guide to field research / Carol A. Bailey.
       p. cm. — (The Pine Forge Press series in research methods and statistics)
    Includes bibliographical references and index.
    ISBN 0-8039-9058-8 (pbk.)
    1. Social sciences—Research—Methodology. I. Title.
II. Series.
H62.B27   1995
300'.723—dc20   94-45023
                                        CIP

About the Author

Carol A. Bailey is Associate Professor in Sociology and the Women's Study Program at Virginia Polytechnic Institute and State University. She has won numerous teaching awards at the department, college, and university levels, including the university-wide Alumni Award for Teaching Excellence. She publishes in the areas of deviant behavior and gender.

About the Publisher

Pine Forge Press is a new educational publisher, dedicated to publishing innovative books and software throughout the social sciences. On this and any other of our publications, we welcome your comments and suggestions.

Please call or write us at:

Pine Forge Press
A Sage Publications Company
2455 Teller Road
Thousand Oaks, California 91320
(805) 499-4224
E-mail: sales@pfp.sagepub.com

*To my mom, Mary Estella Bailey,
my siblings, Margaret, Harold, Rebecca, and Kathryn,
and my "Papy," Carl Leonard Bailey*

Contents

• • • • • • • • • • • • • • • • • •

Series Foreword

The Pine Forge Press Series in Methods and Statistics, consisting of core books in methods and statistics and a series of satellite volumes on specialized topics, allows instructors to create a customized curriculum.The authors of the core volumes are both seasoned researchers and distinguished teachers, and the more specialized texts are written by acknowledged experts in their fields. To date, the series offers the core text in research methods and three satellite volumes focusing on sampling, field methods, and survey research. To be published soon are the core text in statistics and accompanying satellite volumes on such specific topics as regression and data analysis, as well as additional supplementary volumes in research methods.

Carol Bailey's *Guide to Field Research* is designed to assist undergraduate students and other beginning field researchers in carrying out their first qualitative studies. Its rich examples from classic ethnographies, as well as examples generated by the author herself, help bring alive the abstract principles of field research. Drawing on her experience as a field researcher and teacher, the author conveys an accessible yet accurate picture of the subtle realities of doing field research. This volume is streamlined enough to be used in conjunction with Russell Schutt's core text, *Investigating the Social World,* in a basic research methods course. Or it can stand alone as a compact, practical guidebook for anyone who wishes to use field research to answer questions about the social world.

Richard T. Campbell
Kathleen S. Crittenden
Series Editors

Preface

The primary purpose of *A Guide to Field Research* is to give students clear, specific instructions on how to do field research. Unfortunately, I immediately run into trouble in fulfilling this purpose because I think a how-to guide to field research is something of a contradiction. Besides careful record keeping and analysis, field research incorporates luck, feelings, timing, whimsy, and art. I can't teach students how to deal with those things. Nor can I teach many of the characteristics that field researchers need—such as good social skills, ability to cope with ambiguity, and unlimited patience and flexibility. Basically, I believe that if you want to learn how to do field research, you have to *do* field research.

This belief is consistent with the point of a story that first circulated around Harvard many years ago. When a graduate student asked his major professor for some final advice prior to entering the field, the professor, so the story goes, took the largest, fattest field research book off his shelf and said, "Go forth and do likewise" (Nader 1970:98). However, in spite of all the difficulties in trying to write a how-to guide to field research, I'm going to blunder forward, since that is the sort of thing a field researcher does.

A second purpose of this guide is to help students develop analytic tools that they can use for the rest of their lives. By becoming informed consumers of research, students gain the skills needed to evaluate the claims of politicians, advertisers, media pundits, parents, peers, and scientists of all types.

One way I attempt to meet these goals is by focusing in this guide on how doing social research is itself a social product, affected by the same social forces that affect the rest of our lives. The social nature of the research enterprise is often ignored by many of us who teach methods or write textbooks about research. For example, although we teach entire courses on stratification within sociology, those of us who teach methods often act as though the systems of inequality we discuss in our stratification courses are irrelevant to doing research. By understanding that doing social research is a social product, we are better able to do and to evaluate research.

Because I am writing this guide from the perspective of the sociological imagination, my presentation of field research differs (I hope for the better) from the traditional textbook coverage of field research. The first difference is that I emphasize ethical issues in every chapter. Field researchers are simultaneously social scientists and human beings involved in long-term interpersonal relationships in the field. Once field research is rightfully situated in the larger social world, the salience and complexity of ethical issues in field research become acutely visible and can no longer be relegated to a final chapter.

A second difference is that I do not separate the research process from the characteristics of those involved in the research. I emphasize the myriad ways that status characteristics—age, gender, race, ethnicity, sexual orientation, and social class—affect the process of field research. For example, one's race may make gaining entry in one setting difficult but facilitate entry in another setting; one's similarity in social class background with members in the setting may lead to levels of rapport and disclosure that someone from another social class would not be able to achieve. Thus, I argue that what we learn as field researchers is in part a function of who we are.

Third, once field research is viewed as a social process, it is easier to see that field research is not done in a series of stages or steps. One doesn't complete one step or stage and then move on to the next one. Rather, the processes involved in doing field research are overlapping, ongoing, reciprocal, and embedded. Although conventional book publishing techniques require that I present issues in a linear fashion, I stress the synergistic nature of the process.

A fourth difference between this guide and more traditional approaches is that I attempt to highlight the complexities, the ambiguities, the difficulties, and the diverse ways of doing field research. In short, I attempt to give a more accurate picture of the realities of doing field research than is usually presented to beginners. I think hiding academic controversies and internal debates does a disservice to students. Many of us believe a goal of higher education is to help students learn skills for adjudicating differences, resolving conflict, seeing other perspectives, weighing evidence, and valuing diversity. Why do we think we can teach these skills while hiding the messiness within our own academic gardens?

Finally, I hope that I am able to convey in this guide my passion for teaching in such a way as to impart to students a passion for learning.

Acknowledgements

I want to thank many people for their help with this project: Lou Carter and Steve Burkett for first teaching me how to do good research; J. Scott Long for the confidence he showed in me by encouraging me to write this guide in the first place; Amy Crompton and Jill Kiecolt for reading early drafts; and Kathleen Crittenden and Russ Schutt for their concrete suggestions and insights. I would also like to thank the reviewers of this book:

Paul Cromwell, *Miami University*
Barbara Heyl, *Illinois State University*
Kriss Drass, *University of Nevada, Las Vegas*
Jack Spencer, *Purdue University*
Carol A. B. Warren, *University of Kansas*

Additional thanks to the fine staff at Pine Forge Press for responding to all my crises; Steve Rutter for being the perfect handler in these trying times; Meg Korones whose expertise as a copy editor greatly improved the substantive content of this book; Brenda Beck for being good at her profession; generations of field researchers for all that they have taught me; Rhonda Cain, the Texan, for being the best graduate assistant in the entire world; Ed Hogan for always being there and for sharing his joy of language; Eve Doolan, the goddess, whose motivational and editorial skills were absolutely essential to the completion of this project; and Ellsworth "Skip" Fuhrman for providing me with my day-to-day intellectual and emotional sustenance.

A Guide to Field Research

1 The Big Picture: An Overview of Field Research

Betty G. Russell lived with homeless women. She slept in shelters for the homeless, and she ate in soup kitchens. Russell was not homeless; she was a researcher who wanted to understand the lives of homeless women from their perspectives. The methodology Russell used to study homeless women is field research (Russell 1991).

Briefly stated, field research is the systematic study of ordinary events and activities in the settings in which they occur. A primary goal of field research is to understand what these activities and events mean to those who engage in them (Emerson 1988). To gain this understanding, field researchers collect data by interacting with and observing people during the course of their daily lives, usually in some self-contained setting such as a workplace, a street corner, or a place of worship (Van Maanen 1982).

Just as survey research is more than asking a few people a few questions, field research is more than hanging out with, talking to, and watching people. Both methods of research are more complicated and more systematic, with clearly defined procedures to follow. At the same time, field research is flexible, chaotic, emotional, sometimes dangerous, and without rigid rules to guide some aspects of the research process. Art, luck, caprice, ambiguity, and feelings affect the planning, execution, and analysis of field research, making it all the more important for the researcher to be well prepared and trained in this method before engaging in it.

This first chapter gives you an overview of field research. However, it is important to read this entire guide before starting your own field research project. Because field research is not done in stages, you need to fully understand the entire process before beginning your research.

This chapter includes a brief history of field research and a discussion of terminology. Then I introduce you to two themes that are integrated throughout this guide: ethical concerns of field research-ers and the effects of status characteristics on the field research process. I hope that after reading this chapter you will see the big picture clearly so that specific details of field research presented in the rest of the guide will make better sense.

Overview of Field Research

Field research* is the systematic study, primarily through long-term interactions and observations, of everyday life. The goal of field research is to understand daily life from the perspectives of those in the setting or social group being studied. Field research is classified as a longitudinal design because data collection takes a long time—usually months or years.

One of the distinguishing features of field research is where the research is done. During field research, data are collected in the setting of the phenomenon of interest—"in the field." For example, in her study of the homeless (1991), Betty Russell went to homeless shelters instead of asking the homeless women to come to her office. Field researchers go to battered women's shelters, racetracks, television stations, and children's playgrounds. Field researchers observe factory workers, dog catchers, tattoo artists, drug dealers, and flight attendants on the job. Because the field researcher interacts with people on their turf, the people the researcher wishes to observe ideally do not deviate as much from their usual routines as they would if they were participating in an experiment or answering a survey.

Field research is not the only method in which research is done in the field. For example, some types of experiments, called **field experiments**, are done outside the laboratory. During field experiments, researchers often stage an event, such as a rape (Harari, Harari, and White 1985) or illness (Piliavin, Rodin, and Piliavin 1969), in a public place to see how people respond. Also, researchers holding structured interviews sometimes go to people's homes, but during these interviews researchers do not allow any deviation from the predetermined list of questions. Consequently, a major difference between these methods and field research is that the researchers control events and interactions in ways that field researchers do not (Neuman 1991).

---

*Note: **Boldface** terms in the text are defined in the Glossary/Index.

In contrast to controlling the setting, the field researcher attempts to become part of the setting being studied, with the goal of describing the setting in as much detail as possible. The field researcher does this by becoming directly involved with the people being studied and personally experiencing daily life in the setting (Neuman 1991). For example, as part of Russell's data collection, she volunteered for four months at a day shelter. Russell held babies, poured coffee, and chatted with shelter women. This allowed her to observe the residents and the interaction between the service providers and the residents. She observed the women in their roles as residents of the shelters, diners at soup kitchens, participants in social activities, and mothers with children (Russell 1991).

Field researchers engage in this type of research to understand the meaning of daily events from the perspectives of those being studied. The field researcher wants to learn firsthand how the people in the setting live, how they talk, how they behave, and what captivates and distresses them (Emerson 1988:1). For example, Russell was less concerned with how the women became homeless than she was with how they spent their daily lives. She observed the women and talked to them to find out how the women found food, where they bathed and did their laundry, and how they viewed themselves and other homeless women.

Field researchers collect data primarily through interactions and observations. The field researcher interacts with the **members** of a setting as they work, play, worship, eat, and experience life in all its vicissitudes. Field researchers engage in conversations, sometimes called informal or unstructured interviews, with members to gain insights. They observe using sight, sound, touch, taste, and smell.

The interactions and observations of the field researcher are systematic. Field researchers observe at predetermined times, they actively seek out interactions with particular people, they have research questions they hope to answer, and they routinely write field notes. Simultaneously, the interactions and observations of the field researcher are flexible. Field researchers do not have a standardized checklist of behaviors to observe or a predetermined set of questions to ask. Events in the setting often determine the nature of the interactions and what is observed.

Because interactions occur in the course of daily events, the researcher can note trends, document routine events, and understand the meaning of these events (Bailey 1978). Also, field researchers sometimes study how a rare event, such as a hurricane or flood, affects day-to-day life.

In addition to interactions and observations, field researchers sometimes use other techniques to gain insight into a setting. However, because of space limitations and the availability of other textbooks about these techniques, I will mention them only briefly in this guide. Semistructured and structured interviews are common techniques used to supplement observations. Russell held semistructured interviews with 22 women, 10 more than once, and unstructured interviews with approximately 50 to 60 women. Field researchers may analyze the content of documents or give out surveys to some individuals in a setting. Russell includes in her book the results of a survey that she gave to 100 women. Consequently, while field research is classified primarily as a qualitative method, field research reports frequently contain quantitative analyses as well—further blurring the distinction between qualitative and quantitative methods.

The results of field observations are often referred to as **thick descriptions** (Geertz 1973, 1979). Thick descriptions are highly detailed accounts of what was experienced in the field. Many pages of thick description may be generated from a brief interaction. Trying to make sense of this massive amount of data can sometimes be a more difficult task than statistical analysis of quantitative data. Field researchers usually publish their results in the form of journal articles, books, or final reports.

What is ultimately learned from field research is based on the subjective understanding and interpretation of the researcher. Each field researcher brings into the interpretive process his or her own history, personality, training, and status characteristics. As I will explain later in this guide, the status characteristics of the researcher—gender, race, ethnicity, age, sexual orientation, and social class—are particularly relevant to the production of knowledge using field research (Warren 1988).

Unlike most other methods of social science research, field research is highly flexible, done by the lone individual or by a team in conjunction with the members in the field (Wax 1979). It rarely requires hypothesis testing, standardized questions, or manipulation and control of variables. Field research is well suited for, but not restricted to, descriptive or exploratory research. It is often used for generating theory and hypotheses that can be tested later using other research methods.

A classic example of field research is the study done by William Foote Whyte in a slum district of an Eastern city he called Cornerville (1955). He lived there for three and a half years. For part of this time, he lived with a family to get a better view of family life in the Cornerville area. He became a trusted friend of many men and regularly participated in their activities such as bowling, baseball, softball, cards, and just hanging out. At the time Whyte did his study, many academics were writing that slum districts suffered from social disorganization, but Whyte's field research shows that a highly organized and integrated social system existed in Cornerville. For example, he allows us to see through the words of Doc, a leader of one of the street corner gangs, the rules that governed the clashes, or rallies, between rival gangs:

> I don't remember that we ever really lost a rally. Don't get the idea that we never ran away. We ran sometimes. . . . We might scatter, up roofs, down cellars, anywhere. . . . We'd get our ammunition there. Then they would go back to the other end of the street and give us a chance to get together again. We would come out one after another—they would never charge us until we were all out there and ready. Then we would charge them—we had a good charge. They might break up, and then we would go back to our end of the street and wait for them to get together again. (1955:5)

Doc goes on to explain that the rallies were all for fun. In fact, during one rally, Charlie got hit in the eye with a tin can. At that point "the rally stopped," and "after that, there weren't any more rallies" (1995:6). In *Street Corner Society,* Whyte makes an important contribution to understanding urban centers, providing rich, detailed accounts of the daily lives of the corner boys and the college boys who reside in Cornerville. Other examples of traditional field research are the study of urban skid-row inhabitants by James P. Spradley, *You Owe Yourself a Drunk: An Ethnography of Urban Nomads* (1970) and Elliot Liebow's *Talley's Corner* (1967).

Some field research is classified as social critique or activist in orientation. A goal of this type of field research is to provide a benefit or service to those in the setting or social group. For instance, Russell hoped that her book would be used by policy makers to improve the conditions for homeless women. Another example of activist field research is a project that I'm involved in with seven other women. Our purpose is to explore the health care needs of women in Midsouth County (fictional name), which has a wonderfully rich culture but high levels of poverty. In addition to producing professional publications based on this research, we are developing a social marketing campaign and training programs for health care workers to facilitate improved health care delivery in Midsouth County. As one example, we are designing billboard advertisements, based upon what we have learned in our study, to encourage women to obtain free mammograms from the local hospital.

Field research can be exciting or tedious, it can be cheap or expensive, it can be easy or difficult, it can result in the creation of friendships and the loss of relationships, and it can change or reinforce the researcher's worldview. One can rarely predict the fieldwork experience prior to engaging in it. Field research is not for those who need control and structure and who cannot deal easily with ambiguity, creativity, and flexibility (Neuman 1991).

Let's pretend for a moment that you get so excited about field research after reading this guide that you want to learn more. You might start your quest for information by doing a subject search in your library to find books on field research. Most likely you would find very few books that have "field research" in the title. You might continue your search by borrowing some of your friends' research methods textbooks. You would soon note that many of them do not have a chapter called "Field Research." Conversations with your social science professors about field research might confuse more than they clarify. Your frustrated attempts to learn more about field research might lead you to mistakenly conclude that field research must not be a very important form of data collection.

On the contrary, field research has a prominent place in social science research, both currently and historically. The more accurate explanation for your thwarted attempts to learn more is that the "field" of field research is somewhat messy (Denzin and Lincoln 1994). There are debates about what field research is, how it should be done, what it should be called, and when the first field research was done. For example, some say that field research first appeared at the end of the 18th century; others argue that this form of knowledge production existed long before it became the territory of academics. After briefly reviewing some of the history of field research, I will clarify the conflicting terminology and issues that pervade the field research literature.

History of Field Research

Some of the earliest descriptive accounts of social settings date back to the fifth century B.C. In one early account, Herodotus reported to his Hellenic readers that the Scythians collected the scalps of their enemies and made drinking cups from their skulls. The Romans in 37 A.D., the Chinese in the fifth century, and Islamic traders and ambassadors in the eighth century wrote descriptions of other cultures. Field research was done by European explorers, missionaries, government officials, and traders for the first time in the 13th century (Wax 1971). When European trade rapidly expanded into new territories in the 19th century, so did reports written by the traders (Neuman 1991). While touting their work as valid, reliable, and objective, these early works often described "the other" in racist, sexist, and otherwise unfavorable terms.

One of the first sociologists to engage in field research, and indeed one of the first sociologists, was Harriet Martineau. Martineau traveled extensively in the United States in the early 1800s in an attempt to understand everyday life. She paid particular attention to the lives of women and children. As a result of her research, she wrote one of the first sociological guides to field research, *How to Observe Morals and Manners* (1838). She describes in this book the procedures that a social observer should follow in observing and discovering ways of life different from one's own (Fuhrman in press).

British and French field researchers were doing research within their own countries as early as the latter part of the 18th century, with a revival in the latter part of the 19th century. Many of these early field researchers focused on documenting the negative effects of poverty, with the hope that their work would lead to social reform (Wax 1971).

Two of the most well-known researchers during this period were Charles Booth and Beatrix Potter. Charles Booth, a wealthy Londoner, did a systematic study of the working class in London. His field research eventually led to the Old Age Pension Act, which required minimum wages, unemployment insurance, and state coverage for the sick and disabled. One of Booth's contemporaries was Beatrix Potter. Although the daughter of an industrial magnate, she took a job as a sewing machine operator in a London sweat shop. She hoped that by experiencing the working conditions herself, she would be in a better position to document them and to work toward meaningful change (Wax 1971).

Among the first researchers to actually live with the people being studied was British social anthropologist Bronislaw Malinowski in the first quarter of the 20th century. One of Malinowski's main contributions was convincing others that they should do intensive studies of other contemporary cultures by living with the people, learning their language, and experiencing daily life in the culture.

Malinowski, his students, and his colleagues did many influential field studies in the second quarter of the 20th century.

Around the same time in the United States, several sociologists, including Robert Ezra Park at the University of Chicago, were systematically observing ethnic enclaves, religious communities, occupational associations, and mental institutions in Chicago. In spite of the simultaneous growth of survey research and statistical techniques of data analysis, interest in field research quickly spread beyond Chicago and continues to this day (Neuman 1991).

Currently, many researchers are drawn to field research because of the lack of pretense of moral neutrality. Field research has the potential to be transformative—for both the researcher and those in the setting. Consequently, those who have a moral commitment to social change often gravitate to field research (Wax 1971). These field researchers hope to give a voice to society's underclass, to speak on behalf of silenced groups, while knowing that the experiences of others can at best be represented, not captured, by the field researcher. Field researchers attempt to make explicit the influence of class, race, gender, sexual orientation, age, and ethnicity on their representations of everyday life (Denzin and Lincoln 1994).

Terminology

As you can guess from the history of field research, its usage is not restricted to academics or to any one discipline within academia. Different academic disciplines have developed different field research traditions—for example, nursing, education, cultural anthropology, and sociology. Nor is there always consistency within disciplines (Denzin and Lincoln 1994). Further, the standards for field research also have changed historically; the exemplars in the early field research literature are different from those today. At a fundamental level, many aren't sure whether something should be called field research because of *where* the research is done or *how* the research is done. The varied history of field research has led to confusion about terminology.

This section briefly reviews some of the more common terms that appear in the field research literature. This review is not meant to describe all the variants in field research, nor does it imply that one term or conceptualization of field research is superior to another. Rather, my goal here is to familiarize you with enough of the variants so that you won't become lost in the morass if you decide to pursue this topic further. Although this guide is limited to one specific type of field research, be aware that there are many legitimate variants of this methodology.

Field study refers to any study that is done in a natural setting. For example, field experiments and field research are both considered field studies because they are done in natural settings, although the techniques of data collection for the two methods are different from each other.

Fieldwork is sometimes used interchangeably with field research, but it more accurately refers to that part of field research that is done in the field. When you finish your data analysis in the comfort of your dorm room, you are still engaged in field research. However, since you are no longer in the field, the fieldwork portion is considered complete.

Ethnography or **ethnographic study** is a method developed by cultural anthropologists; these terms are often appropriately used interchangeably with field research. An ethnography describes a culture and gives meaning to the description. The goal of ethnography, as with field research, is to uncover both the tacit and the explicit cultural knowledge of group members being studied (Neuman 1991). The choice between the terms *ethnography* and *field research* is more an artifact of disciplinary training than a reflection of a difference in method.

Discourse-based field research focuses primarily on face-to-face interactions among members in a setting. Much of the methodology for discourse-based field research is similar to what is covered in this guide, such as ways of gaining entry and getting informed consent. However, discourse-based field researchers focus on how members construct their social worlds through talk. Discourse-based field researchers tend to use audio- and videotape recorders rather than field notes or interviews used by more traditional field researchers.

Observational studies collect data on nonverbal behavior by using sight, hearing, taste, touch, and smell. In observational studies, one observes behaviors rather than asking respondents about their behaviors. Sometimes field research is inappropriately listed as a subtype of observational studies. Observations are a major part of field research. However, field research frequently includes other forms of data collection, primarily involvement in daily activities and informal interviews with members. Thus, field research is a broader category than observational studies.

Many authors classify field research as **participant** or **nonparticipant observation** to indicate the degree to which the researcher actively participates in everyday events in the field setting. The participant observer takes part in daily events while observing; the nonparticipant observer observes but does not take part in routine activities and events in the setting. Some authors use a fourfold table to describe the level of involvement—complete observer, observer as participant, participant as observer, and complete participant (Gold 1969; Junker 1960). Some suggest three categories of participation, while others conceptualize the degree of participation as a continuum, without discrete labels for a particular location on the continuum.

Scholars further classify research by whether those in the setting are aware of the researcher's dual roles (participant and researcher). If the members in the setting are aware of the dual roles, the research is classified as **overt research**. If those in the setting are not aware of the dual roles, the research is classified as **covert research**. Covert research is particularly controversial; a discussion of ethical issues related to covert research follows.

The debate over how and whether to label one's level of participation is part of the larger debate over what counts as field research. For example, some argue that being only an observer and not a participant is possible and is a legitimate form of field research; others say that field research must include the researcher's full participation in the setting. It is not my task to resolve this debate; however, there isn't space in this guide to cover all the legitimate variants of field research. Therefore, I restrict my discussions in this guide to field research in which the researcher actively participates at a variety of levels with the members in the setting. In other texts, this variant might be referred to as ethnography or overt participant observation.

Ethical Issues in Field Research

Ethical considerations are an important part of field research. As I will demonstrate throughout this guide, ethical issues permeate every aspect of the field research process, from selecting the research topic to disseminating the results. The prolonged and personal interactions with those in the setting during field research create the possibility of myriad ethical questions without easy solutions. Although professional organizations have ethics codes that members are required to follow, field researchers have not always agreed on a set of ethical standards.

To begin to sensitize you to the salience and complexity of ethical questions in field work, I discuss in this section two major ethical concerns of field researchers: deception and confidentiality. Field researchers hold diverse ethical positions regarding these issues.

Let's begin our discussion of ethics with a classical example and a question to ponder. Laud Humphreys (1970) studied men who engaged in homosexual acts in restrooms in public parks by acting as a lookout for the men. Humphreys then recorded the men's license plate numbers and used these to obtain their names and addresses. Wearing a disguise, he went to these men's homes and interviewed many of them, often without being recognized. Setting aside the ethics of his observations in the parks, let's concentrate on the interview portion of his research. Was it unethical for Humphreys to disguise himself, hide how the subjects were selected, and not give the true purpose of his study to the men during the course of the interviews?

The issue of **informed consent** is salient to answering this question. Many researchers consider informed consent an important component of ethical research on human subjects. To get informed consent, the researcher must make those being studied aware of the following:

1. That they are participating in research
2. The purpose of the research
3. The procedures of the research
4. The risks and benefits of the research
5. The voluntary nature of research participation
6. The participants' right to stop the research at any time
7. The procedures used to protect confidentiality

Only after the subjects understand each of these and agree to participate can the research continue. In some cases, signed informed consent forms are required.

Whether informed consent is a requirement of ethical field research is still debated among academics. On one side of the debate are those who argue that **deception** in field research is acceptable. Proponents of this perspective argue that informed consent is not necessary and may be counterproductive in field research. One justification offered by this group is that because field research takes place in a natural setting, with little manipulation and control over those being studied, there is little potential for harm.

Another justification for using deception is that some research might be impossible without it. Informed consent may lead to so much **reactivity** that the research becomes meaningless. Jack Douglas, a proponent of this position, believes that the social researcher is "entitled and indeed compelled to adopt covert methods . . . in order to achieve the higher objective of scientific truth" (Douglas 1979:17).

A third rationale for using deception is that a certain amount of dishonesty is routine in social interactions. Rarely do we expect those with whom we interact to be completely honest. In fact, the completely honest person is often seen as hurtful and lacking in social skills. Gans writes:

> If the researcher is completely honest with people about his activities, they will try to hide actions and attitudes they consider undesirable, and so will be dishonest. Consequently, the researcher must be dishonest to get honest data. (1962:42)

Those who defend deception argue that both people with and without power attempt to hide the truth.

A more fundamental critique of informed consent provided by proponents of deception is that in practice informed consent protects the powerful under the guise of protecting the powerless. That is, if deception is not used, researchers will be denied access to the very groups that social scientists have an ethical mandate to study. This group asserts that one duty of social scientists is to "uncover corrupt, illegitimate, covert practices of government or industry" (Galliher 1982:160). Van den Berghe took this position during his research in South Africa. He writes:

> From the outset, I decided that I should have no scruples in deceiving the government. . . . The question is, how much honor is proper for the sociologist in studying the membership and organization of what he considers an essentially dishonorable, morally outrageous, and destructive enterprise? (van den Berghe 1968:187)

Finally, those who argue that informed consent is not necessary weigh the benefits of the research against the potential risk. In the case of Humphreys, they would consider the benefits of his research in relationship to any harm he may have caused. If his deception allowed him to gain data that would have been impossible with informed consent, and there was minimal harm, then his actions were not unethical.

On the other hand, many do not find deception acceptable. Several variants of this position appear in the literature. Given the current acceptance by many field researchers of the **feminists'** arguments against deception, even among those field researchers who do not call themselves feminists, I will concentrate on this variant in the following discussions and throughout this guide. However, note that many field researchers adhered to these principles long before feminists began articulating them.

One of the first rules of medicine is "Primum non nocere." This translates to "First do no harm." This could also be one of the first ethical rules of feminist field research. Using a broad view of harm adopted by some feminists, an ethical field researcher should not: (1) harm those being studied, (2) harm the setting, (3) harm the researcher himself or herself, (4) harm the profession represented, or (5) harm the reciprocal relationships formed in the setting.

A premise of a feminist ethical stance is that the process and outcomes of field research are greatly affected by the reciprocal relationships that develop between the field researcher and those in the setting (Sieber 1982). The field researcher shares the emotional pains, secrets, fears, hopes, insecurities, strengths, and accomplishments of those in the setting. In return, the field researcher might offer support, compassion, encouragement, advice, and even love. People in the setting also share and respond to the thoughts and emotions of the field researcher.

These reciprocal relationships form the moral basis of ethical decisions relating to field research among those who take a feminist ethical stance (Sieber 1982). Because researchers expect those in the setting to be honest with them, the reciprocal nature of the relationship is harmed if the researcher engages in deception; therefore, field research that employs deception is considered unethical. In spite of the important insights that Humphreys gained from his interviews, those who adhere to a feminist ethic would most likely consider his lack of honesty during research unethical.

Deception also interferes with rather than facilitates understanding in a setting. For example, the researcher may be convinced that by using deception he or she can experience what members are experiencing, although this actually is not the case. Let's return to Betty Russell to illustrate this point.

During her research on homeless women, Russell pretended for three days to be homeless by dressing like homeless women, eating with them in the soup kitchens, and spending nights in a shelter for the homeless. While I admire her concern for the homeless, I argue that her days of living as a homeless woman resulted in only a superficial understanding of the experience. I suspect the mental anguish of knowing one has nowhere else to go and the uncertainty of not knowing when homelessness will end are crucial elements in the experience of homelessness. Homelessness is more than just a physical experience. The chronic stress of prolonged homelessness cannot be experienced in a brief experiment—especially when one knows that the condition of homelessness can be changed at any moment. If Russell got too cold, too scared, too hungry, or too tired, she could have stopped her research and returned to her own comfortable world. The homeless cannot do that. Therefore, it would be incorrect for Russell to assume that her three-day experience was equivalent to the experience of a truly homeless person.

Realistically, it is naive to think that we can succeed at deceiving those being studied in a field research setting. While it is possible to do field research in a setting where one is a member prior to the research, this is not often the case. In most instances, the researcher is an outsider. The researcher often differs in age, social class, educational level, skin color, grooming habits, body language, religious affiliation, country of origin, customs, and worldview. Most group members will be aware that the researcher is new to the setting; consequently, deceiving the members about the researcher's dual role is probably not possible. For example, in our research in Midsouth County, my midwestern accent immediately identified me as an outsider whenever I spoke. In addition, the small community made it likely that any lie I told as to why I was there would have been checked and found to be false. Rather than conceal my purpose, I openly communicated my research role and desire to participate to most of those with whom I came into contact. For the most part, community members were flattered to be of research interest and were willing to talk, include me in events, and show me around. Not being truthful would probably have lead to suspicion, resentment, getting caught in a lie, and lack of cooperation—not to mention my own tension about lying to my new friends.

Deception also may prevent insight. Rosalie Wax expresses this thought when she writes:

In many cases, the finest insights of the fieldworker are developed from interaction within the self. . . . This interaction is constricted and distorted when the researcher is preoccupied with sustaining a fraudulent presence. (1971:52)

Because I did not have to hide who I was in Midsouth County, my mind was free to listen, question, and observe.

Another argument against deception is that most people allow researchers to ask certain questions, such as those that are stupid or blunt, that are not allowed of insiders. For example, in Midsouth County the women at the housing project were clearly aware of my research interest in health care issues. It seemed completely appropriate for me to ask what they do when they get yeast infections. A question on yeast infections would not be easy to casually work into a conversation if my interest in women's health concerns were not explicit, and thus valuable information would have been unobtainable. Part of what was learned from these conversations will be incorporated into our educational campaign in Midsouth County.

The role of researcher also allows one to go places that otherwise might be taboo. For example, outsiders are not always welcome in Midsouth County, due partly to the history of tension and violence between the outside representatives of coal companies and local union members. When I explained my concern for women's health and my background, their legitimate suspiciousness toward outsiders was reduced, and I was welcome in most homes. The fact that I came from a background of rural poverty—my home when I was growing up did not have running water or an inside toilet—was an asset. It is doubtful that I could have overcome their mistrust of outsiders if I had attempted any other role than what I was—a concerned researcher.

As you begin to plan your research, you need to think about your ethical position. Fortunately, students can get help in resolving some ethical decisions prior to the start of their research. Colleges and universities are required to review all research involving human subjects. Consequently, you will need to write a research proposal and submit it to your instructor; your instructor will give it to the appropriate committees. An important part of this proposal is a discussion of whether informed consent will be given, how, and to whom. If you want to engage in covert research, you should clearly justify why you think your deception will be harmless to those studied, to yourself, to the profession, and to the norm of reciprocity. However, it is unlikely that review committees will grant permission for research that contains deception. Therefore, you would be wise to design a project that does not require deception and to explain your procedures for informed consent. Later in this guide, I will discuss some of the practical issues involved with informed consent in field research.

Another important ethical issue is confidentiality. Ethical researchers need to inform those in the study whether the research is anonymous, confidential, or neither. Research is **anonymous** when the researcher is not able to identify the participants in the study. In a **confidential** study the researcher knows or could know the identity of the participants but does not reveal who they are. Sometimes participants in research agree to allow their identities to be disclosed. Most field researchers work under conditions of confidentiality, and this confidentiality must be strictly guarded for the research to be ethical.

Researchers risk violating confidentiality when they are tempted to verify or get people's reactions to statements made by others. Field researchers must train themselves not to give in to this urge because it is common for members in a setting to talk about each other. John Van Maanen had this experience while doing field research on police:

> Even among my confidants, talk was more readily forthcoming about someone else's patrol unit, squad, shift, or division. People are apparently far more willing to disclose the secrets of others than they are their own. As a result, I learned from some policemen that all traffic officers are rule-minded zealots more fond of motorcycles than of their wives, that all narcs are on the pad, that good sergeants are invisible sergeants, that live beats are full of deadbeats, that black officers are more loyal to their black brothers than to their blue ones, and so on. (1982:116)

If Van Maanen had attempted to verify these opinions, he might have violated the confidentiality of his sources. Fortunately, field researchers are relieved from the tasks of verification and triangulation. Because we are interested primarily in what subjects believe to be true, and because ultimate truth is sometimes a questionable concept, we avoid violating confidentiality by not confirming the accuracy of most statements.

Breaking confidentiality can cause harm to members—which is a serious ethical violation. For example, in our research in Midsouth County, members of a grassroots organization told us that they secretly hired a water expert to determine if their drinking water was safe. They did not want the water board to know that they were independently testing the water. If we leaked their plans, the water board might have made temporary adjustments to make it look as if the water was safe when it wasn't. We could have seriously damaged their cause to get safe water in Midsouth County if we had disclosed this information before the tests were done. Another example from Midsouth County was the admittance by some of the health care professionals that they occasionally lied on government forms in order to help their clients receive needed medical care. The supervisors of these individuals might not have found this practice laudable.

Keeping confidentiality becomes particularly problematic when authorities think the researcher has knowledge of law violations. Here's an example. Rik Scarce, a graduate student at Washington State University, was doing research on animal liberation activists. Authorities contacted him, trying to obtain information about a suspect in a raid on a laboratory at Washington State. Not only did Scarce not reveal the content of any interviews, he even refused to testify about whether he had any confidential research interviews with the suspect. As a result, Scarce was sent to jail. His case may go to the U.S. Supreme Court before it is decided ("Eco-warriors" 1990).

Although the legal issue is not resolved, the social science community has incorporated clear guidelines into their ethical codes. For example, the American Sociological Association requires that researchers maintain confidentiality even when this information enjoys no legal protection or privilege and legal force is applied (American Sociological Association 1994). To meet the ethical guidelines of most academic professions, all those who take part in the research need to know whether and how their confidentiality will be protected. If you think keeping the results of your research confidential might be problematic—ethically, legally, morally, socially, or physically—then it is best not to do the research.

Not everyone who does field research would agree with this advice. Such disagreement is illustrated in this exchange between Wolfgang and Sagarin and Moneymaker. Wolfgang suggested that if researchers have "doubts about a moral obligation to violate the rubrics of confidentiality" they should absent themselves from involvement in this kind of research (1976:31). Sagarin and Money-maker respond:

> Not always is this information known, a priori. And excellent as this may be as a guideline for keeping out of trouble, it is hardly of equal standing for doing first-rate research. (1979:190)

It is not always easy to know in advance when keeping confidentiality might be a problem, but this is more likely in some settings than in others. I advise students to do "first-rate research" by avoiding field research that places them in a setting—such as a criminal subculture—where they are likely to observe (and be pressured by members in the setting to do) behaviors that powerful groups would want them to report.

Unfortunately, the issues pertaining to protecting confidentiality are more complicated than simply dealing with outside sources who pressure you to break it. Sometimes researchers get into situations where they believe they have a moral and legal duty to violate confidentiality, although as researchers they have promised not to do so. For example, in John Van Maanen's ethnography of a U.S. police department, he recorded the following incident in which two police officers, Barns and McGee, throw Blazier, a suspect, into the police van.

> From outside the van I can hear the very distinct smack of wood meeting flesh and bone. After perhaps a half minute or so, Blazier, thoroughly dazed and maybe unconscious, is pulled from the wagon, bounced to the pavement, handcuffed, and tossed back in. . . . In the prowl car, Barns remarks; "What a place to try to put somebody out. It's so f___ing cramped and dark in that van you don't know what's going on. I kept hitting something with my stick, but I didn't know what it was until I heard that creep's glasses shatter. Then I kept hitting the same spot until I felt it get kind of squishy." . . . This episode was neither the most violent nor the most blatantly questionable police incident I have observed in the course of my studies. (Van Maanen 1982:137)

Barns and McGee know that Van Maanen is a researcher. They also know that they have been promised confidentiality. However, a man's life is at stake. Laws may have been broken by the police officers. Should Van Maanen report this incident? If he does, he will probably not be able to continue his research. Is documenting the brutality and publishing the results more important than this one incident? There is no easy answer to these questions. Like Scarce, Van Maanen was later served a subpoena to testify and turn over his field notes on the Blazier incident. For a variety of complicated reasons, Van Maanen attended the hearing as required but refused to testify or turn over his field notes.

How to resolve these dilemmas is unclear. Confidentiality is required by professional organizations, but the law—and your own moral stance—requires disclosure in many such instances. Sometimes intervention can be a partial solution. Intervention is not prohibited by either professional organizations or the law. One choice Van Maanen could have made was to attempt to stop the beating when it was happening. Intervention might have been better for Blazier. However, because intervening might lead to the end of police cooperation, and thus end the research, it is not a panacea to ethical problems either.

Part of the debate on confidentiality revolves around issues of power—the power of those doing the harm versus those being harmed. Some argue that it is unethical to break the confidentiality of the powerless—such as prostitutes, children, and poor people. Along the same lines, some argue that if the powerless are being harmed by powerful groups or institutions then confidentiality should be broken. Bulmer takes this position:

> Specifically social scientists are seen as having a responsibility to study those institutions or government agencies that are in a position to mistreat the disadvantaged, and if evidence of wrongdoing is discovered on the part of government officials or administrators, it should be publicly disclosed in an effort to discourage future wrongdoings—regardless of any promises made to the public officials to respect confidential information, their anonymity or privacy. (1982:210)

Think about the Blazier case. Blazier was a relatively powerless man who was beaten by powerful agents of social control. Using Bulmer's arguments, Van Maanen had an ethical duty to break his promise of confidentiality to the police officers.

Others argue that status characteristics, such as the amount of power individuals have, should not be a consideration in ethical decisions. Everyone should be treated equally. However, this is hard to do in practice—and not everyone agrees that it is a desirable goal. Let's use the Blazier example to see whether you believe that everyone should be treated the same. How important is confidentiality of the police officers if Blazier is a murderer who got off on a technicality? If Blazier is a black man with a drinking problem? If Blazier is one of your college friends? If Blazier is your female relative? If Blazier is the son of the governor of your state? If the police officers are your friends or relatives? In summary, do you think status characteristics should affect how individuals are treated during research?

Status Characteristics and Field Research

Sociologists frequently look at the effects of **status characteristics**—gender, race, ethnicity, social class, sexual orientation, and age—on life experiences. A large body of empirical evidence indicates that status characteristics structure nearly every aspect of everyday life. One's gender is related to such things as one's occupation, one's wages, whether or not one is interrupted when talking, and one's risk of interpersonal violence. For example, women tend to be clustered in fewer occupations than men; women's wages are lower on average than men's, even for the same work; women are more apt to be interrupted in mixed groups than men; and women have a greater risk of rape than men but a lower risk of being murdered. Other status characteristics similarly shape individuals' experiences. For example, race and ethnicity are correlated with place of residence, quality of educational experience, job opportunities, health care, and risk of violence. Sociologists argue that status characteristics help locate individuals within a hierarchical social structure, and location within the social structure affects one's resources, responsibilities, and opportunities.

Given the impact of status characteristics on everyday life, it should not be surprising that these characteristics are important in field research. We are finally starting to acknowledge the myriad ways in which status characteristics matter in virtually all aspects of social research (Warren 1988). This section illustrates some of the ways status characteristics affect field research by focusing on gender. However, similar arguments can be made for race, ethnicity, sexual orientation, social class, and age. These issues are dealt with in more detail throughout the guide.

A basic organizing category of social life is gender. Unlike one's sex, which is primarily a biological classification, gender is a social construction. Gender includes the social and psychological components associated with being male and female. Consequently, definitions of gender are highly variable across cultures and time.

As the definitions of gender have changed, so too have the definitions of who should do field research. During certain periods, for example, field research was viewed as an appropriate method for women because it was primarily "an intuitive/emotional qualitative method"; men were thought to be better suited for "logical/objective quantitative work." This does not mean, however, that women's participation in field research was valued. For example, the field research of female scholars in the early 1900s such as Ruth Benedict, Elsie Clews Parson, Hortense Powdermaker, and Ellen Churchill Semple did not receive as much attention as that of their male counterparts (Bailey 1994).

Changing definitions of gender and a concern for gender equality have also resulted in more field research being done on settings of concern to or about women. For example, the numerous studies of homeless men are now joined by studies of homeless women by Rousseau (1981), Weiner (1984), Crystal (1984), Russell (1991), Liebow (1994), and others.

With the new focus on women, there has been a renewed commitment to research that benefits women and minorities. Field researchers are working with and for a variety of groups that have traditionally been ignored, such as people who have AIDS, welfare recipients, the homeless, and urban youth.

An emphasis on equality has also expanded the methods of field research. When social science was more androcentric and less egalitarian, field researchers were trained to be rational and objective (traits associated with men) and to avoid emotionalism (a trait associated with women). With the recognition of women and women's experience has come an appreciation of feelings as well as cognitions in field research. Consequently, in addition to the **positivist research tradition,** which has a commitment to objectivism, value-free science, and reliability, many field researchers adhere to an **interpretive model,** which holds that there is no objective reality independent of the social meaning given to it by those in the setting.

The emphasis in the rest of the guide will be on how gender affects the outcomes of field research. In brief, when one is doing field research, one engages in gendered interactions, gendered conversations, and gendered interpretations (Warren 1988:10). One's gender affects what aspects of a setting one will come to know and the interpretation of experiences. Thus, gender affects the production of knowledge.

Clearly, attention to gender issues does not simplify to a question of whether men or women are better at field research. In spite of stereotypes of women as empathetic, it is a myth that women are naturally better at field research. It is equally untrue that only men are capable of good scholarship. Nor are gender issues as simple as whether a woman or a man is safer in a particular setting, although this is an important concern. Rather, an analysis of the gender/field research nexus is much broader. A complete review of gender and field research would need to address how changing definitions of gender have corresponded with who does field research, how it is done, what is considered worthy of study, what is learned, and for what purpose.

It is insufficient, however, to focus only on the way social research is "gendered." We all simultaneously have a race, social class, sexual orientation, age, and other characteristics that affect the research. That is, one does not have either a gender or a race; one has both— and a sexual orientation, age, and social class background as well. Field research is also affected by these combinations of status characteristics. A theme throughout the remainder of this guide is to help you become aware of the complicated ways in which the combination of status characteristics affects every aspect of field research, from gaining entry to what is written in the final report. I have included in the appendix an article by Matthews Hamabata that I think does an excellent job of pointing out how status characteristics affect the field research process.

This chapter has provided you with an overview of field research and an introduction to the themes of ethical issues and status characteristics. You may have correctly surmised from this chapter that a "how-to" guide to field research is somewhat of a contradiction. Field research requires a great deal of flexibility, without rigid rules to guide many aspects of the research process. Nonetheless, the chapters that follow present suggestions derived from generations of field researchers for you to use as a flashlight, rather than a map, throughout your journey into field research.

CHAPTER HIGHLIGHTS

1. Field research is the systematic study of ordinary events and activities in the settings in which they occur.

2. The goal of field research is to understand what these activities and events mean to those who engage in them.

3. Interactions with members in the setting, including observations and informal interviews, are the primary means of collecting data in field research.

4. The field researcher's experiences are recorded in the form of field notes and analyzed for a publication or final report.

5. Field research is an interpretive process—each researcher's interpretation is influenced by his or her biography and status characteristics.

6. Field research has a long and important history within the social sciences.

7. There is disagreement over what field research is, how it should be done, and what the different types should be called.

8. Ethical issues in field research are complex.

9. Not all field researchers agree on what is considered unethical during field research.

10. A feminist ethic requires that the reciprocal relationship between the researcher and members of the setting be the moral basis for ethical decisions.

11. Most researchers agree that ethical research requires informed consent and that no harm be done to members of the setting, to the researcher, to the profession, and to the relationship between the researcher and members of the setting.

12. Keeping promises of confidentiality can be difficult for the field researcher.

13. Status characteristics affect virtually every aspect of the field research process: what is learned during field research is not independent of who one is.

EXERCISES

1. Use each term presented in this chapter in the section on terminology as the key word for a library subject search. How many books do you locate for each term? Read the titles. Do you see any patterns in the types of books you are finding using the different terms?

2. Imagine that you are doing field research on a high school program that is designed to help students at risk of dropping out of high school. This program is not particularly well received by the community. In the course of your research, you discover that the

guidance counselor for this program is having a sexual relationship with one of the students. Should you tell anyone? Discuss how those who hold different ethical positions would handle this situation, and then decide what you would do. Be sure to discuss the implications of the various decisions (Fetterman 1982).

3. Reread the section on the Blazier incident. As an ethical researcher, what would you do if you observed this interaction? Does your answer depend on the status characteristics of Blazier? Does your answer depend on the purpose of your research? That is, what would your decision be under the following conditions?

   a. You are doing the research for a class project.

   b. You were hired by the police to do the research.

   c. You were hired by the ACLU to do the research.

   d. You are doing the research because you have a professional interest in the topic, and you need a publication.

4. John Van Maanen reported on an incident in which the police threw a boy about 10 years old to the pavement and verbally assaulted him because the child "had aimed a ceremonial upright third finger in the direction of the passing patrol car" (1982:137). Van Maanen felt that the police reacted as they did partly because of his presence in the car. Discuss the ethical issues involved in this incident and possible ways of responding.

5. Discuss the myriad ways that your college experiences are affected by your particular combination of status characteristics. Be sure to discuss both the privileges and the costs of having a particular configuration of characteristics.

6. Paul Atkinson and Martyn Hammersley write the following:

   All social research is a form of participant observation, because we cannot study the social world without being part of it. (1994:249)

   What do you think they mean by this statement? What are the implications of their statement for those who classify field research on the basis of the level of participation? Do you agree or disagree with Atkinsons and Hammersley's statement? Justify your answer.

7. Read the article by Matthews Hamabata that is included in the appendix. Write down all the ways that status characteristics affected his research.

2 In the Beginning: Starting a Field Research Project

When I was in graduate school, my professors often said "The methodological/statistical tail should not wag the theoretical dog." This phrase was supposed to remind us that our theory should determine the research methods and statistical techniques used and not the other way around. When we were given this advice, we were being trained in the dominant model of science.

This chapter begins with an overview of that dominant model of science. Then I hope to give you a realistic picture of why field researchers do field research. I provide some suggestions for selecting a research project, deciding the preliminary goals of the study, and preparing for the research. I reiterate in this chapter the two themes I introduced in Chapter 1. First, ethical issues are always a concern in field research. Second, field researchers need to be aware of the effects of status characteristics throughout the research process. I also introduce a new theme in this chapter: Field research does not proceed through discrete stages.

The Dominant Model of Science

In many textbooks, the dominant model of science is represented by a wheel or circle such as the one shown in Exhibit 2.1. The process of scientific discovery supposedly proceeds clockwise around the "wheel of science." The researcher begins with a theory. Using deductive reasoning, the researcher derives a testable hypothesis from the theory. Then data are collected to test the hypothesis. Based on the results of data analysis, one decides whether there is empirical support for the hypothesis. The right half of the wheel—from theory to data collection—is called deductive research. The purpose of this type of research is usually explanatory or theory

Exhibit 2.1

The Research Wheel

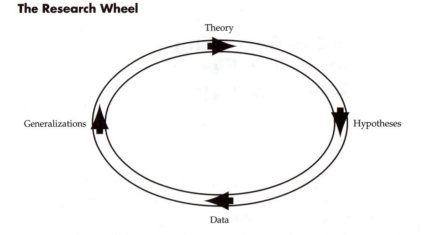

testing. Some researchers believe that a model of social science like the one in Exhibit 2.1 is the only legitimate way to do research.

Here is how you might do research if you were following this model of the scientific process and were intrigued by a theory of chess players' behavior that you read in a journal article. Upon some reflection, you would derive a testable hypothesis about chess players from this theory. Next, you would decide on the appropriate method for testing your hypothesis—collecting survey data, designing an experiment, doing a content analysis, or engaging in field research. Once you made this decision, selected your sample of chess players, and obtained informed consent, you would collect your data. After analyzing your data, you would decide if you found support for your original theory of chess players' behavior or if your theory needed to be modified or rejected. Others might repeat your work, testing their hypotheses on different samples of chess players. Eventually you would hope to have a good theoretical understanding of the behavior of chess players through the process of theory testing and modification.

The wheel in Exhibit 2.1 also represents inductive research. During inductive research, the researcher enters the wheel at the point of data collection and travels up the left side of the wheel. The researcher collects the data and then extrapolates from the data insights into human behavior. That is, the researcher makes general statements about social life from specific behaviors that he or she observed. The general statements, or insights, derived from the data are called **generalizations.** When a theory is developed inductively, it is called **grounded theory** because it is grounded—it has its base in specific observations of social life (Glaser and Strauss 1967). In addition to generating theory, the purpose of inductive research is often exploratory or descriptive. However, most field researchers choose an inductive method because they believe that field research is the best way to understand the social world.

If you were following the inductive model, you might realize that all those weekends that you are spending at chess tournaments might be a valuable source of data. You decide that you want to do field research on this setting because you find chess players a fascinating group and you want to understand them better. You engage in systematic observations and interactions with chess players over a long period. Based upon the field notes from your research, you write and publish the theoretical ideas that you have developed from the data.

Obviously, the wheel is an oversimplification for pedagogical purposes of how real research is done. Research is not either deductive *or* inductive but contains elements of both. Research is not theory testing *or* exploratory but contains elements of both. Research that starts as theory testing can end up primarily descriptive. Some research, such as that designed to bring about social change is not easily illustrated on the wheel. Further, one study on a topic, whether deductive or inductive, is never enough—life and social science are too complicated for a full understanding of the social world to be gained from one study. Therefore, social scientists seek insights into the social world through the cumulative effect of their work. The "wheel of science" is traveled many times in complicated patterns by researchers who hope that each time the circle is traveled we come closer to understanding our social world.

Social scientists hold contrasting views about what it means to understand the social world. Those who subscribe to the tenets of a **positivist model** argue that there is a truth or objective reality waiting to be discovered by social scientists. The researcher discovers this reality and the general causal laws that govern human behavior by staying detached, neutral, and objective throughout research.

In contrast to the positivist model of science, many current field researchers subscribe to an **interpretive model** (Emerson 1988:vii; Geertz 1973). An interpretive model says there is no objective reality to discover independent of the social meaning given to it by those in the setting. In addition, an interpretive model assumes that even those in the same setting may not experience social and physical reality in the same way. Consequently, it is only through inductive reasoning and an interpretive model that a researcher can hope to reveal the meanings, values, and rules of living used by people in their daily lives (Neuman 1991).

Some scholars believe that this interpretive framework is the foundation of field research. They argue that a researcher must engage in "active, empathetic participation in the rounds and structures of life and meaning of those being studied" (Emerson 1988:2) in order to label the research as field research. Field research is classified not solely on where it is done but by the distinctive interpretive way in which the research is done (Emerson 1988). Although this is consistent with the definition of field research that I am using in this guide, I want to remind you that other definitions of field research do not include an interpretive framework.

Some field researchers combine elements from a **critical perspective** with elements of an interpretive model of research. Field researchers who use a critical approach tend to do activist research. These researchers want to document, understand, and change the way that powerful groups oppress powerless groups. A goal of much of this research is to empower the people in the setting to work toward meaningful social change (Neuman 1991).

Selecting a Project

Scholars select field research for a variety of reasons. Sometimes academicians decide to do a field research project for a change from their routine activities. Alternatively, they might find that they have access to a unique setting, and the opportunity to do field research is just too good to pass up. Agencies or individuals sometimes hire or provide grant funds for an experienced academic to do field research in a particular research setting. Mostly, however, field researchers select this method because they believe it is the best way to understand a variety of settings and social groups.

Some of the settings and social groups that have been the focus of published field research include the following:

- Support groups for the caregivers of Alzheimer's disease (Gubrium 1986)
- A residential treatment center for emotionally disturbed children (Buckholdt and Gubrium 1979)

- A chapter of Gamblers Anonymous (Livingston 1974)
- Upper-level drug dealers and smugglers (Adler 1985)
- A nonprofit tax-exempt membership corporation that offered classes, workshops, and individual counseling in health-related fields (Kleinman 1980)
- Women in outlaw motorcycle gangs (Hopper and Moore 1994)
- Genital piercing, branding, burning, and cutting (Myers 1994)
- The subculture of bodybuilding (Klein 1994)
- The economic crime unit within a county prosecutor's office in a midwestern state (Gurnery 1982)
- The anti–nuclear power movement (Downey 1986)
- Organized criminals (Ianni 1972, 1974; Klockars 1974)
- Fat admirers (Goode and Preissler 1990)
- Gamblers at horse races (Rosecrance 1990)
- A self-help group for affective disorders (Karp 1994)
- The punk counterculture (Fox 1994)
- A Scientology group (Wallis 1977)

Some of my students have done field research projects on these settings or social groups:

- A local sewage treatment facility
- A church where members handle snakes as part of their religious rituals
- A rural grocery store where dances are held on Friday nights
- The College of Engineering
- Video game stores in the local mall
- A bingo parlor
- A health clinic that specializes in incontinence
- Sky divers
- A junk yard
- A bakery

They also have done field research in the library, dorm cafeterias, more than a few local bars, and other settings familiar to college students. One student, who was concerned about the criteria used by the Student Budget Board for deciding which student activities and groups should get funded and which shouldn't, obtained permission and did her field research during the monthlong budget hearings.

I suspect many of you have been assigned a field research project, and you need to decide what to do. Obviously many different settings and social groups are appropriate for field research, so how are you going to choose? The follow sections discuss some issues that you should consider when selecting a field research project. You need to go back and forth among the issues raised, rather than proceeding through them in the linear fashion in which they are presented in this guide. The issues raised are not discrete steps to proceed through but are interrelated like different–colored yarn in an afghan. Regardless of where you start or end up, self-reflection about your worldview will be part of the process of selecting a field research project.

Worldview

Ideally, researchers select fieldwork projects that they consider important and in which they have an ongoing interest; chance occurrences and practical issues also affect such decisions. One's perspective or worldview affects what one considers important or interesting. This perspective is intimately connected to one's values and to one's status characteristics. Sometimes, but not always, one's perspective is associated with a recognized and explicit theoretical position such as a feminist, functionalist, or symbolic-interactionist theoretical perspective. An example might help illustrate how a particular worldview can be used to generate research ideas.

Many researchers are concerned with making the lives and contributions of women and minorities visible. Sometimes this means exploring "women's settings or social groups" that previously have been ignored or studied from a perspective that reinforced the second-class status of women. Jennifer, a student in one of my classes, was concerned because many of the experiences of women and minorities go unnoticed. She also liked sports. Therefore, she did a field research project on the college women's softball team. Because the women's softball team received minimal funding and lacked the attention given to even the women's varsity basketball team, it fit her perspective of "rendering the invisible visible."

Our involvement as researchers with the Midsouth County health care project is derived from a combination of critical and feminist theoretical perspectives. We are concerned that the women of Midsouth County are not getting adequate health care because of the inequalities in the U.S. health care system; many of these women do not get routine pap smears, prenatal care, or mammograms—things that many women take for granted. Therefore, working with the women of Midsouth County to improve their health care is a rewarding way for us to spend our time and is consistent with our theoretical perspectives of documenting and eradicating inequality.

James P. Spradley (1970) articulates his worldview in the first chapter of his classic ethnography of urban nomads. He believes that is is possible and desirable to change institutions in the United States to make them more responsive to our multicultural society. He writes the following about changing our institutions:

> But they can only be renewed effectively, renewed so that they serve *all* members of our nation, if we have a full appreciation for the pluralistic, multicultural nature of American society. Americans do not simply belong to different generations, classes, racial or ethnic groups. They have also acquired distinct values, goals, and life styles—they come from different subcultures. America is faced, not simply with an urban crisis, but with a grant experiment in human community: can we create a society which recognizes the dignity of diverse culture patterns? Can we renew our institutions so they are truly human with the full realization that there are a variety of ways to be human? (1970:4–5)

Because Spradley feels that the first step in answering these questions is to understand American subcultures, he did a field study of urban men, primarily living on skid row, and their encounters with law enforcement agencies for public drunkenness. He hopes that by understanding the men from their point of view we might become more accepting of difference.

Not all of you will have a recognized and explicit theoretical perspective. Some of you will have an idiosyncratic, implicit, and personal worldview (Fetterman 1982) developed from a combination of common sense, folklore, ideology, craft knowledge, and religion (Berger and Luckman 1967). Nonetheless, whether you realize it or not, you most likely have a worldview of some sort. Having a worldview, whether explicit or implicit, helps us create accounts, descriptions, and explanations of our social world. These allow us to function and make sense of our experiences. Your perspective will most likely influence your selection of a research project, and it certainly will affect your observations and interactions within the setting. Consequently, while field research is rarely designed to test a particular theory, virtually every aspect of it is influenced by one's theoretical perspective or worldview.

If you have trouble articulating your worldview, self-reflection might help you identify an important field research project. Take some time to think about what interests or concerns you. Sometimes it helps to ask yourself questions such as these:

- Do you want to make the world a better place to live in?
- Would you like to know about the everyday world of people who are a lot different from yourself?
- Is there a particular group that you have been curious about but haven't explored?
- Can any of your current hobbies, roles, and activities be a fruitful setting for a field research project?
- Are you fascinated by religion, crime, small businesses, or sports?

Answers to these sorts of questions can help you think about possible settings or social groups. You may find that, as the research proceeds, you are able to identify your perspective.

Feel free to generate as big a list of potential projects as you can. The list will be trimmed as you consider the other important issues involved in selecting a project.

Ethical Issues

One goal of project selection is to select projects that are ethically well grounded. While you cannot predict all the ethical issues that could possibly arise from your choice of a field project, you can minimize such problems by asking yourself a series of questions before selecting your project.

First, can the research that you are considering be done without deception? Deception becomes a possibility when you think that members in the setting will change their behavior enough to make the research meaningless as a result of your presence. If you think this will be the case, you should select another project to avoid the temptation to deceive.

Second, how difficult will it be to keep promises of confidentiality? As discussed earlier, confidentiality issues are more problematic during research on illegal, immoral, or unethical behaviors. Can you in good conscience promise confidentiality to a social group whose behaviors you want to expose? Can you keep confidentiality if your methods professor insists on knowing where the research took place? You might want to consider the worst possible scenario related to confidentiality and decide whether you think you could handle it before proceeding with a particular project.

Third, what are your chances of getting **dirty hands** while engaging in this research? Getting dirty hands refers to engaging in illegal behavior or behavior that is against your own moral standards during the course of the research. You need to be particularly careful about illegal behaviors because engaging in research cannot be used as a legal defense for breaking the law. Is the possibility of getting your hands dirty a serious enough concern for you to select another project? For example, how likely is it that someone may encourage you to use a drug that you normally wouldn't use?

Fourth, will your research give tacit approval to a setting or group that you consider to be unethical or illegal? For example, if there is a group on your campus that actively discriminates against blacks, would you be able to research this group and disassociate yourself from the group's racist policies? What might you do, for example, if this group decided to attend a march sponsored by the Ku Klux Klan? You might gain some valuable observations by joining the march, but your presence would show support for racism.

Fifth, what are the chances that your research will harm anyone in the setting? Even if you keep confidentiality, can your presence in the setting be distressful to group members? For example, if you decide to study a group of mothers receiving Aid to Families with Dependent Children, would your presence make these mothers feel somehow "unfit" or "different" in spite of your reassurances to the contrary? Might your final report bring unintended negative consequences to group members?

Sixth, could the project cause you any harm? How might your project affect your reputation? Imagine, for example, that you do your field research project at a location that is known for being frequented by prostitutes. What could this potentially do to your reputation if acquaintances routinely saw you come and go from this location, but they did not know your purpose? Being unfairly associated with a group does not necessarily mean you shouldn't do the research. In fact, having a legitimate excuse to associate with different subcultures is sometimes part of the appeal of field research. However, if you are easily hurt by the opinion of others, you need to keep that in mind when deciding whether to proceed with a project that might affect your reputation.

Also consider your personal safety. Will you be safe getting to and from the setting? Will you be safe in the setting? Physical safety issues are particularly salient for women and sometimes minorities. Simply being an outsider can increase your risk in some situations.

These are just a few of the ethical issues to ponder as you select a field research project. As with most aspects of field research, there is not a complete list of ethical issues to consider—nor is there a rule book on how to resolve ethical issues in project selection. Think about as many ethical issues in advance as you can and make your best decision. Talking about these issues with your class instructor is also wise.

Social Setting/Social Group

Field research project selection also involves determining if you are interested in a particular setting or a social group. For example, some field researchers want to understand the dynamics that take place in a particular setting or site, such as an abortion clinic, crack house, or children's playground. Other researchers are interested primarily in particular social groups, such as construction workers, Red Cross volunteers, sorority members, or the lesbian community on campus. In these latter cases, the fieldwork portion of the research most likely would not be confined to one setting. Rather, the researchers would observe the group members as they move in and out of a variety of sites.

In practice, a distinction between a setting and a social group is often nonsensical. For example, if you wanted to do field research on alumni tailgate parties at football games, you are interested in alumni as a social group but not in a variety of settings—only in the site of the parking lot before football games. However, thinking of social settings and social groups as distinct classifications is sometimes a useful way to come up with a greater number of potential field research projects, and it also may help clarify your research goals.

Practical Issues

There are numerous practical issues to consider in selecting a research project. One important issue is time. Do you have time to get to and from the setting? Do you have the flexibility to make the observations during different times of the day and night? Is this the right time of year for the project? For example, a major social event at Virginia Tech is tubing down the New River. While a field research project on this setting would make sense in late spring and summer, fall and winter are not appropriate times for this research. Do you have enough time to do thorough observations and interactions and still finish the project by your deadline? For many class assignments, you need a project that you can complete in days or, at most, weeks—not months or years.

Your training as a researcher is also important. Do you have the research skills needed to do a thorough job? That is, at your level of training, do you think you can do justice to the setting you are interested in?

Do you have adequate financial resources for the task? Can you afford to get to and from the research setting and pay for your food and shelter while you are there?

Will you be physically safe in a particular setting? Do others' responses to your race, ethnicity, gender, age, or sexual orientation put you at additional risk?

You also need to think about your personal resources. If you are extremely shy, you might want to avoid settings where interacting with strangers would be a frequent requirement. However, you need not always avoid settings in which you might feel uncomfortable. Wonderful research has been done by researchers who are not only uncomfortable but downright miserable in a setting. For example, Eleanor Miller (1986) wrote that overcoming her fear was part of her motivation to continue her research on women involved in crime. However, you need to complete the research, and you won't if you end up in a setting that requires more in resources than you are willing or able to give.

Accessibility

Another important question in project selection is access. Sites range from open—requiring no permission to enter—to closed—requiring permission to enter. Most public areas such as local parks, swimming pools, libraries, are open. You do not have to obtain permission to be there, although you still need to decide whether your research will be overt or covert. At the other extreme are closed private settings such as offices, homes, and elementary schools. Some settings have laws and regulations that restrict access. Even when channels are available for obtaining permission, the procedures can increase the time required to complete the project. So in selecting a research project, consider whether you need to gain advance permission to enter the setting and if you have the time and resources to obtain permission.

Field researchers sometimes find that they are not allowed in a particular setting because of their status characteristics. If you are of the "wrong" gender you might be denied access to numerous activities, roles, and locations designated as appropriate for only one gender (Warren 1988). Restrictions can also be based on other status characteristics such as age, sexual orientation, race, ethnicity, or religion.

Even if you can gain access to a setting, those in the setting may restrict your observations and interactions within the setting because of your status characteristics. For example, if you were doing field research on Mormons, you would not be able to observe some religious rituals unless you were a member of this church. Sometimes a combination of status characteristics is used to restrict access. For example, it is not surprising that Peggy Golde (1986) was not accepted in the world of men during her study of the Nahua Indians of Mexico. However, the fact that she was unmarried and childless also prevented her from being fully accepted in the world of adult women.

The Familiar versus the Unfamiliar

There are mixed opinions on whether it is better to do field research in a familiar or unfamiliar setting. Some argue that if a person already understands the dynamics of a setting from the members' perspectives, then there is little need to do research in this setting. Beginning researchers are usually advised to do research in unfamiliar settings because it is easier "to see cultural events and social events" in an unfamiliar setting (Neuman 1991:344).

Others argue, and I tend to agree, that familiarity with a setting or group provides a firm foundation upon which to build. Those who are familiar with a setting may already have rapport with members, understand the nuances of language and behavioral expectations, and have analytic insights into the working of the setting. It is sometimes the case that the only person who has a chance of being allowed to do research is someone who is already known to the group. This was the case for Columbus Hopper and Johnny Moore (1994), who studied women in outlaw motorcycle gangs.

Prior to the work of Hopper and Moore, women's involvement in motorcycle gangs was virtually ignored. Hopper and Moore's study provided details on such things as the place of women in biker culture, the rituals they engage in, the women's role as money-makers, and their motivations and backgrounds. Hopper and Moore were able to do this study only because this was a familiar setting. They write:

> The main reason we were able to make contacts with bikers was the background of Johnny Moore, who was once a biker himself. During the 1960s, "Big John" was president of Satan's Dead, an outlaw club on the Mississippi Gulf Coast. He participated in the rituals we describe, and his own experience and observations provided the details of initiation ceremonies that we related. As a former club president, Moore was able to get permission for us to visit biker clubhouses, a rare privilege for outsiders. (1994:391)

An important contribution to our understanding of women's participation in motorcycle gangs would have been lost if Hopper and Moore had followed the advice not to study familiar settings.

Size

The size of the setting and social group are important considerations for the beginning researcher. Although field research has its roots in studying entire cultures, studying an entire culture is not recommended for the undergraduate who needs to complete a project by the end of the term! A reasonable social group size for beginning researchers is 30 or fewer members, and the setting should not cover too much territory. Relatively limited spaces are good choices: tattoo parlors, weight rooms, beauty salons, or doctors' waiting rooms are all appropriate settings (Neuman 1991).

Documenting Your Decision

Project selection is not an antecedent to field research but rather is an integral part of it. Why and how you select a particular setting or social group affect everything that follows. Consequently, you need to document the selection process in great detail.

Let's illustrate how selecting a project becomes part of the research. Pretend that you have a burning curiosity to understand interaction patterns in laundromats. Your field setting is going to be a laundromat—but which one? You have access to several laundromats. As you check out your options, you may find Duds & Suds more interesting than Cook's Cleaners. You may have learned from a cursory visit to Cook's Cleaners that it is primarily used by college students with little diversity in age and social class. In contrast, you noticed that Duds & Suds is used by a wider age range of participants, small children are frequently present, and the social class of the users is more varied. As you evaluate the two laundromats you feel that there would be richer data available in Duds & Suds.

It is important that you document your observations and how they affect your decision while you are making the decision. Do not assume that you will remember your decision process. You won't! You are going to be bombarded with input. Picking one laundromat instead of another has a major effect on what you observe, so be sure to make careful notes about your selection process; these field notes will become a crucial part of your analysis and final report.

Sometimes decisions are made for very practical reasons, such as picking a laundromat because it is close to your home. This doesn't make you a bad researcher; but hiding or ignoring the implications of the multiple decisions made throughout the research process might. Field research is self-critical and open. It requires that you give the details—even if they aren't always pretty.

As you decide which laundromat to study, no doubt your mind will race with other thoughts related to your research. You need to document these as well. As you do so, you may refine your project selection and delineate the goals of your research. To continue with the laundromat example, you might become curious about whether a visit to the laundromat is seen as a break in the workday, a chance to sit down and socialize, or another of many dreaded tasks to be completed in limited time. As you write these thoughts down you notice that you are less interested in laundromats than you are in how mothers of young children negotiate multiple demands upon their time. The laundromat becomes only one of many settings in which multiple demands occur. Through the process of documenting your choice of Duds & Suds instead of Cook's Cleaners, your research project changes from a concern about the setting of laundromats to a concern about mothers' experiences in laundromats.

Goals of the Study

On one hand, deciding on the goals of field research is easy. Almost all field researchers have the same goal—to understand social interactions within the setting or social group from the perspectives of the members. On the other hand, the goals of the study can be as broad as your imagination.

In addition to the desire to understand daily life, researchers usually enter the field with a series of goals specific to their study. Without at least some preliminary goals, field researchers would be overwhelmed with the task of observing everything and talking to everyone about everything.

I will illustrate preliminary goals by using four examples from the published field research literature. In her study of homeless women, Betty Russell was interested in "to what extent homeless women have developed a specific culture or subculture" (Russell 1991:4); this goal is consistent with the broad goals of most field researchers. However, she also had a list of specific questions to focus the study:

> Once a woman was without permanent shelter, what strategies did she use to survive? Where did a woman find food? What arrangements did she make for shelter? Where did she obtain clothing? Where did she bathe and launder her clothing? How and where did she fill the hours of her days? What possessions did she take with her when she became homeless? How did she view the agencies with whom she came in contact? How did she view herself and other homeless women? What were her hopes, fears, and dreams? What attitudes did she bring with her from the mainstream, and what attitudes did she change? (1991:4)

Was it Russell's interest in these questions that led her to study homeless women? Or did her interest in homeless women lead to these study goals? Maybe both processes occurred simultaneously. As noted in the previous section on project selection, the goals of a project often develop concurrently with the task of choosing a project. For practical purposes, it doesn't matter which comes first—particularly since one's goals frequently change during the course of the research. What is important is to document the process of selecting and changing goals.

As a second example, consider the goals from a joint field research project done by Robert Prus and Styllianoss Irini (1988). They were interested in understanding the daily lives of the hotel community—hookers, strippers, bartenders, cocktail waitresses, bouncers, desk clerks, bar patrons, and rounders. More specifically, they delineated three goals. First, they wanted to understand the interrelatedness of these different groups. Second, they wanted to understand how individuals in the groups managed their careers. Finally, they

were interested in the interpersonal relationships in the hotel setting—such as friendship, loneliness, sexuality, and violence. It took
these two researchers over three years before they felt they had met
their goals. It is difficult to guess how long their research would
have taken if they had not reduced their goals to these three!

Although John Van Maanen was not very specific in the goals he
articulated prior to his study of a U.S. police department, he is now
somewhat embarrassed by how his early goals expressed his naiveté
and a "little loathing, some fear, and considerable curiosity" he had
toward the police (1982:107). This is what he wrote at the start of his
research:

> What is the key to this analysis is the process which so success-
> fully converts a basically mindless and floating young man into
> a cool, calculating tool to be manipulated toward ends which
> are neither representative of the individual cop's long-term
> interests nor of the larger society's interest. What is of interest
> then is the identification of the elements of the well-oiled and
> well-funded machine that cranks out cops in increasing num-
> bers. The aim will be to put together in as bias-free manner as
> possible, a detailed examination of the forces at work which
> combine to manufacture our blue-shirted, homogeneous mass
> of storm-troopers. (1982:107)

The fact that Van Maanen's perception of the police—and thus his
goals—changed repeatedly during his years of research is typical.
What makes Van Maanen so exemplary is the degree of honesty and
self-reflection that he provides about his work. Van Maanen uses a
hint of humor to express how his views changed during the course
of his research:

> Upon reading my early notes from the luxurious position of
> having been to and from the field several times, certain changes
> in attitude and perspective are obvious to me. I now wonder
> just who that 26-year-old person writing such notes was and
> what in the world was he doing running around using my good
> name? (1982:107)

Elliot Liebow also changed his goals during the course of his research. He realized that he had a new aim for his study of homeless
women as he was analyzing his field notes. He writes:

> Tell Them Who I Am focuses on the dynamics of shelter life. Ini-
> tially, my aim was to write a straightforward description of shel-
> ter life and, ideally, to try to see the world of homelessness as

homeless women see and experience it. Later, when trying to make sense of my notes, I realized that another of my aims was to explain both to myself and others how these women remained human in the face of inhuman conditions. (1994:1)

Changing goals during one's research is OK. In fact, being able to change goals as one proceeds is one of the big advantages of field research over many other methods. However, at least minimal goals need to be delineated at the start of the research to provide a focus for the research. As goals change, the good field researcher reflects about the changes and documents the reasons for the changes and their implications.

In summary, field researchers try to be open and receptive to the group being studied and not enter the setting with specific hypotheses to be tested. However, the field researcher should identify at least a few goals of the study before the research begins and refine them as the research progresses (Fetterman 1989).

Preparing and Gaining Skills

Even though the field researcher rarely has a theory to test, she or he does not enter the setting with an empty head. The more the researcher knows before entering a setting, the more he or she can learn while there. Therefore, I suggest that you learn about a setting by thoroughly reviewing the literature before entering the field. However, some disagree and suggest that the review of the literature should wait until one has left the field. Either way, all agree that a review of the literature is important.

Review of the Literature

When looking for relevant literature, you should read field research by others who have studied your particular setting or settings similar to yours. For example, if you want to do field research at a pawn shop, you might learn a lot by reading ethnographies of tattoo parlors, junkyards, and head shops. Sometimes newspaper accounts, autobiographies, surveys, historical accounts, and even novels can be useful in helping you to prepare emotionally, physically, and intellectually, for field research in a particular setting.

Before giving you some hints on how to go about finding the literature that you need, I'll tell a brief story. Recently when teaching research methods I had students write in as much detail as possible how they would go about doing a thorough review of literature on a given topic. The answer that amazed me the most was written by a college junior. He wrote, "I'd walk around the stacks in the library until I found a book on the topic." While he may indeed be able to find a book on his topic using this method, it certainly is not the most efficient approach! Fortunately, most students have a much better idea of how to locate books in a library. However, if you do not know how, ask for assistance at your library.

My experience tells me that there are two areas in which many students can use a bit of advice about locating books. First, many students have not learned the benefits of section browsing. Books are shelved (in most libraries) by similar subjects. If you go to a particular section to locate one book, browse through the books near the one you were looking for. A glance at the table of contents or index of a nearby book will tell you whether you have found an additional treasure. Exploring a small section of the library that you know contains relevant subject matter is not the same as wandering the stacks.

Second, many students are unaware that they can look for relevant books not owned by their library. The old-fashioned way to do this is to use a source that lists all published books, such as *Books in Print*. Now many colleges and universities have computerized databases to help you search for all the books on a topic. Some of these databases, such as PSYCHLIT, will even search tables of contents for you. These computerized databases are most likely located in the reference section of your library.

If you use one of these databases and find a title that you want to read, copy the complete citation for the work. Then using the card catalog or the computerized equivalent, check to see if your library owns this book. If your library does not own a copy, the interlibrary loan department may be able to help you. Interlibrary loans give you access to thousands of libraries and are usually free although it may take several weeks for books to arrive.

While most of you are probably familiar with locating books, some of you may not have had as much experience with locating journal articles. Journals are an important way for scholars to disseminate the results of their research. Thousands of journals are published; any individual journal will have a fairly narrow focus. For example, *The International Journal of Eating Disorders* publishes articles about eating disorders such as bulimia nervosa. Some journals have a slightly broader focus, such as *Social Forces*, which publishes articles on many different topics written from a sociological perspective. Some journals that frequently publish field research are the *Journal of Contemporary Ethnography, Qualitative Sociology, Deviant Behavior: An Interdisciplinary Journal,* and *Qualitative Inquiry.* By looking though these journals you can see interesting examples of quality field research.

As with books, it is inefficient to find the journal section of your library and browse until you find something interesting. Relevant journal articles are located using indexes and abstracts or the computerized equivalents. The *Readers Guide to Periodicals* will not help you find most journal articles; it is more appropriate for locating articles in magazines, not journals. Computerized journal databases such as PSYCHLIT and SOCIOFILE are thorough and efficient ways of locating journal articles. For some topics, INFOTRAC might be an additional database to explore. A librarian can tell you what computerized databases your library owns and how to use them.

A subject search of one of these databases will tell you how many articles have been written on your topic and give you the complete citation of the articles. Databases also allow you to read the abstracts of articles at the comfort of a computer terminal, thus saving valuable time by eliminating irrelevant articles. If you do not know how to locate journal articles using abstracts, indexes, or CD-ROM computerized databases, ask a reference librarian. Once you become skilled in using the library, you will wonder how you ever survived without it.

Final Preparations

When explaining to students the importance of preparing for the field, I use Herbie Goldfarb as an example. Herbie Goldfarb is one of the characters in the book *The Milagro Beanfield War* (Nichols 1974). Herbie arrived in Milagro as a VISTA volunteer without sufficiently preparing for the task. Herbie did not speak Spanish (the language of Milagro); he failed to bring warm clothes because he thought the Southwest would be hot all the time (he hadn't realized there were snowcapped mountains in the Southwest); and he shared a one-room "house" with snakes, skunks, and black widow spiders because he thought living arrangements had been made for him (they weren't). In order to avoid being a Herbie Goldfarb during your field research, you need to prepare.

Think about clothing and the weather. Wear shoes that are comfortable for walking and standing because you may be doing more of this than you are used to. If there is any chance that you will spend time outdoors, prepare for rain, wind, or snow (Neuman 1991; Fetterman 1982). If you will be spending time indoors, do not assume there will be good heat or air-conditioning. Plan accordingly. You also need to know how the members in the setting dress. This does not mean that you need to sprout a leather jacket for doing field research on a motorcycle club. However, blue jeans and a T-shirt would be appropriate clothing.

For some locations, the prepared field researcher packs personal items such as toilet paper or menstrual products. Check to see whether you should bring your own food and water. Do not assume that there are 24-hour restaurants or gas stations available in rural settings or urban centers.

You will need to obtain the research supplies that you will be using in the field. Notebooks of various sizes are a staple for field researchers: small ones for discretely jotting down field notes in public, larger ones for transcribing your notes each evening if you do not have a computer or typewriter to use. Make sure you have several pens and pencils. Maps or diagrams, index cards, scissors, folders, and variously sized envelopes or cardboard boxes are wonderful for collecting and organizing materials that you will be accumulating. Many field researchers use tape recorders. If you are going to be in the field for long periods, have a second recorder available and more high-quality tapes than you expect to use. One can never have too many batteries; if you are using a camera, take along extra batteries for it too. Pack a variety of films. Some field researchers like to use video cameras, which require their own tapes, batteries, and cords. Portable computers (with all the accessories—battery packs, extension cords, and so on) are extremely useful for creating field notes, but the cost still makes them a luxury. In lieu of a computer, a typewriter, lots of paper, and correction fluid will do. You will need to create multiple copies while in the field, so you need to find an onsite copier, take your own printer, or pack carbon paper for typing multiple copies as you go.

Even sites that are close to home require advance planning. For example, if you are going to do your research at the combination laundromat and bar Pub 'n Suds, you will need coins to feed the parking meters and washing machines and strategies for managing come-ons from other patrons. You may need to take snack food if you are observing the local bus station and a seat cushion if observing the crowd in the bleachers at a baseball park.

In addition to all these things, field researchers need the skills of careful observation, short-term memory, and regular writing (Neuman 1991:343). These skills can be sharpened. Before beginning your research, develop your skills by regularly observing, listening, and taking field notes as you go about your everyday life. Keeping a personal journal also may help you develop this important aspect of field research (Neuman 1991). Finally, typing your field notes with either a typewriter or a computer is much better than writing them by hand. If you do not know how to type, learning how before going into the field is well worth the investment.

A last note about preparation. Be aware that Murphy's Law frequently operates in field research: If something can go wrong, it probably will. Consequently, field researchers often mentally prepare for this by being willing to be flexible, to adjust, and to make compromises in their original plans. Field researchers often subscribe to the German expression "Glück im Unglück," which means "fortune in misfortune." Field researchers need to turn unfortunate events into advantages.

Thomas Parkhill was able to do just this. His original goal was to get to the town of Ramnagar in India so that he could study the *Ramlila*, an important religious event. Parkhill never made it to Ramnagar, but he did a wonderful study of *Ramlilas* in smaller neighborhoods instead. He writes:

> Arriving in Banaras in early autumn, 1984, I intended to follow other scholars from the West across the Ganges River to study the Ramnagar *Ramlila*, a religious drama of widespread reputation. Determined to learn how a religious story was treated in a performance context, I spent the first days of the *Ramlila* season negotiating the river currents and the sometimes soggy Ramnagar geography. One afternoon, after I'd literally missed the boat to Ramnagar, I began to explore my own neighborhood and discovered a *Ramlila* there. (1993:103)

As a result of his willingness to adjust, Parkhill made an important contribution to understanding the Hindu religion through his work on neighborhood *Ramlilas*. However, Parkhill's work on neighborhood *Ramlilas* was not without further complications. Although he was able to visit 14 *Ramlilas,* many of them up to four times, his observations of the *Ramlilas* ended abruptly when the *Ramlila* season was cut short by the assassination of Indira Gandhi on October 31, 1984.

Institutional Review Board Approval

Even though most professional organizations have their own codes of ethical conduct, the U.S. Department of Health and Human Services has issued regulations designed to protect the human subjects of research. Under these regulations, every college and university is required to have an **institutional review board (IRB)**. The IRB reviews research proposals to ensure that the research meets ethical guidelines. For example, the IRB staff makes sure that informed consent is obtained, that there will be no physical or psychological harm to the subjects, and that adequate procedures will protect the confidentiality of the subjects. Before beginning your research, you will need to get IRB approval.

At most colleges and universities IRB approval is obtained in stages. Although the procedures vary from one institution to the next, most follow this pattern. Your instructor gives you the IRB forms. You answer the questions on the form and provide a copy of your research proposal. Your instructor reviews your IRB request and has you redo any problematic parts. Then your instructor forwards your request to the head of your department. If this person approves, your request is sent to the institutional review board, which makes the final decision. Field research in public places is often exempt from IRB guidelines; however, you still need to file the forms in order to receive the exemption. Once you have IRB approval (or exemption) you can proceed with the fieldwork portion of your research.

As you read the next chapter, which discusses fieldwork, remember that the issues discussed there are not independent of the issues just presented in this chapter. For example, you will need to present your preliminary goals to the gatekeepers; what you pack for taking field notes will make a difference in how inconspicuous you can be while taking them; and how you handle informed consent will have to be part of your institutional review board petition. Consequently, although these chapters are separated in this book, the issues covered in them are not separated during the actual practice of doing field research.

CHAPTER HIGHLIGHTS

1. Field research is usually classified as inductive; it follows an interpretive model and is done because field researchers think it is the best way to understand the social world.

2. Many factors influence project selection including one's worldview, ethical and practical issues, accessibility, size of the setting and the group, and familiarity with a particular setting or group.

3. Project selection is an integral part of field research, so the decisions involved in project selection need to be thoroughly documented.

4. Creating specific goals for a study is an important part of getting started, although these goals can be modified during the research.

5. Field researchers need to prepare mentally and practically for the demands of field research and for unavoidable changes in plans.

6. A literature review is an important part of field research.

7. Field researchers need to obtain institutional review board approval before starting their research.

EXERCISES

1. Browse through recent journal articles. Find one that is primarily deductive, one that is primarily inductive, and one that is not easily situated on the traditional "wheel of science." Discuss in detail how well and what elements of each article match the components on the "wheel of science."

2. Locate and read one of the examples of published field research given in this chapter. Write a summary of the major points of the work. Include the relevant methodological details in your report.

3. Pretend that you are an instructor for a research methods class. A student wants to do field research on a campus group whose purpose is to work for the legalization of marijuana. Discuss all the pro and con factors that should be considered during selection of this group as a project setting.

4. Betty Russell and Elliot Liebow both studied homeless women. Compare the goals of these two researchers. Are they the same or different? What questions and types of observations would these two researchers need in order to meet their goals?

5. Someone says to you, "I've decided where I'm going to do my field research. Now I'm done with that step and can move on." How should you respond as a field researcher?

6. Pretend that you want to research one of the settings or groups mentioned in this chapter. Write a proposal to obtain institutional review board approval for your study.

3 Getting to Know You: Data Collection in the Field

If I asked you to talk about your college experiences, no doubt you'd spend a lot of time discussing your relationships with others. Your relationships are probably the most wonderful and sometimes the most painful components of your college life. Daily you engage in relationships of various degrees and types. You may have a close romantic relationship with a significant other. You probably have some formal and fairly distant relationships with some of the faculty and staff. You have informal, positive relationships with other students. Sometimes your relationships might be negative, as with an ex-roommate. You may have relationships that serve an explicit function, such as when you work with others on a class project. No doubt the dynamics of your many relationships change constantly and greatly affect how you perceive the quality of your day-to-day life.

Just as your relationships delimit and define your college experiences, relationships delimit and define the field research process. The unifying theme of this chapter is the care and maintenance of field relations. Watch for the implicit and explicit importance of relationships in the topics covered in this chapter—gaining entry, obtaining informed consent, working with key actors, establishing rapport, and doing observations and interviews. Participating in relationships with the members in the setting is the basis of the interpretive process that is so central to field research. These relationships are the foundation of what field researchers come to know in the setting.

Gaining Entry

Remember our friend Herbie Goldfarb from *The Milagro Beanfield War* (Nichols 1974)? Herbie was excited about being in Milagro, so he assumed the members of the community would be as eager to have him there as he was to be there. This was a false assumption in

Herbie's case, as it often is in field research. Herbie might have been more successful in Milagro had he known some of the procedures that successful field researchers use to gain entry to a setting.

Gaining entry is a complicated process, and the particular route one takes to gain entry affects the rest of the research. For example, procedures for gaining entry depend on the location of your setting and whether you are doing the research alone or with others (Burgess 1991).

As noted previously, not all settings are open to everyone; some require permission for entry. The individuals who play a key role in granting or denying access are referred to in field research literature as **gatekeepers**. Formal organizations (such as schools, hospitals, prisons, and businesses) invariably have formal gatekeepers whose permission you must obtain. Many public areas (such as public waiting rooms and local parks) do not have gatekeepers. In between these two extremes are informal gatekeepers. These are people who do not have institutional power but nonetheless have informal power over your fate in a setting (Neuman 1991:345).

In addition to controlling access, gatekeepers control the flow of interactions within a setting (Burgess 1991). Gatekeepers dictate when the researcher gets to come and go, who is talked to for how long, and what can be observed. They also decide what data and information are available to the researcher (Burgess 1991). Consequently, the gatekeeper has a great deal of power in dictating the parameters of a study.

Sometimes inexperienced methods instructors teach students that all they need to do to gain entry to a setting is to obtain permission from the person highest in authority. Unfortunately, this advice grossly oversimplifies the process of gaining entry for several reasons.

First, while permission from the top is necessary, it is usually insufficient to ensure cooperation from all those involved. Field researchers need to seek permission and reassure the gatekeepers at every level (Dean, Eichhorn, and Dean 1969). It is a mistake to believe that there is only one gatekeeper for any research site (Burgess 1991). Many settings have both formal and informal gatekeepers.

Second, it is not always best to begin with the person at the top. Doing so can lead to gates being closed at lower levels. For example, people lower in authority may assume that you have been sent to report on them by those at the top, and this assumption may lead to at best superficial cooperation.

Third, gaining entry to a setting is more than just being given permission to do the research. Gaining entry is part of the research process, not something that precedes it. The interactions established during entry profoundly affect what follows (Dean, Eichhorn, and Dean 1969).

Finally, gaining entry is usually negotiated and renegotiated throughout the research process (Burgess 1991). Johnson aptly describes the process of gaining entry as a continuing, "progressive series of negotiations rather than a one-shot agreement" (1975:176).

At every stage of discussions with gatekeepers, help establish your credibility by being honest. Explain who you are and why you are doing the study. For those of you who will do field research for a class project, a letter of introduction written on departmental stationery from your instructor might help you in some settings. Make it clear why you are doing the research; for example, explain to the gatekeepers whether your research is a class assignment and whether you hope to publish the results. Tell the gatekeeper whom you'd like to share your field notes and the final report with, and ask if this is acceptable. If your research is sponsored, that is, if someone is paying you to do the research, you need to let the gatekeepers know (Dean, Eichhorn, and Dean 1969). It is a breach of ethics to hide the source of research funding.

Gatekeepers need a reasonable explanation of the goals of your study to help them decide whether to grant you entry. If your goals for doing the research are not clear, this greatly increases the chances of being denied access. Be prepared to explain how your goals of wanting to understand the day-to-day interactions in a setting are different from wanting to evaluate or judge the setting. It helps to practice in advance what you intend to say to the gatekeepers (Dean, Eichhorn, and Dean 1969); however, you also need to be flexible because you will probably need to negotiate your goals with the gatekeepers. Also, informal gatekeepers need to understand the goals of the research; remember that each person in the setting is "to a greater or lesser degree a gatekeeper" (Burgess 1991:48).

Let's use our imaginations again to illustrate some of the issues involved in gaining entry. Pretend that you have a long-time interest in what goes on behind meat counters in grocery stores. In order to do research in the meat department of a local grocery store, you probably will need to obtain permission from the store owner, the manager of the meat department, the union representative, and the workers themselves.

Where you begin seeking entry depends upon the context. If you happen to know one of the workers in the meat department, you might start by obtaining permission from this person and his or her coworkers. Then you could ask this person to introduce you to the union representative, who in turn will approach the department manager on your behalf. If you do not know a worker, you might begin with the store owner and proceed from there.

If the store owner and the department manager think that you are using research as a guise to determine if inferior meat is sold or if they are exploiting the workers, it is not likely that they will grant you permission. Nor will the union representative and the workers in the department make you welcome if they think that you have been sent as a management spy. Listing clear research goals will help allay some of the suspicion.

Gender is an important factor to consider when getting permission to enter a setting. Field researchers of the "wrong" gender find that they are denied access. For example, women may find it more difficult to get permission to study settings that are dominated by men, such as professional sports teams, business clubs, or junkyards. Alternatively, a group dominated by a particular gender may view a researcher of the other gender as a delightful addition to the setting, making it easier for the researcher to obtain permission.

Just as your gender can work for or against you in complicated ways as you attempt to get permission to do your research, so can your race, ethnicity, age, sexual orientation, and social class. For example, a heterosexual woman wanting to research lesbian reading groups might be warmly welcomed by some groups and not welcomed by others. Remember, too, that often people react to the intersection of these characteristics. For example, just because you know someone of your gender has done research in a setting, do not assume that you will automatically be welcome—particularly if your race, ethnicity, age, sexual orientation, or class is different from the previous researcher.

Sponsorship

It is important to inform field research participants and gatekeepers if the research is being sponsored. That is, they need to know if someone else is paying to have the research done. Having a sponsor can affect the relationships between the field researcher and those in the setting in complicated and not always obvious ways.

Robert Burgess (1991) relates an example of how **sponsorship** affected his research. He was hired by school board members to do field research in district schools. Although the local teachers could not deny him access to their classrooms because the school board had granted him permission, his presence was less than welcome. The teachers resented the fact that the school board funded his research project but would not fund much-needed clerical help for them. Consequently, his relationships with the teachers were negatively affected by the sponsorship, but he would not have been able to do the research without the school board funding.

Another important aspect of sponsorship is the relationship between the sponsor and the researcher. When someone else pays for the research, the research topic and research questions are often developed in conjunction with the sponsor. In addition, sponsors will sometimes attempt to direct how the research is done, even though they may have little or no training in field research. Field researchers are sometimes put into the bind of having to decide between doing research that is influenced by others and not doing research at all.

Another important area of negotiation between the researcher and the sponsor is data ownership. All involved must clearly understand who will see the raw data, who will read the finished report, and who controls publication and dissemination of results, including things such as conference presentations, publication, and newspaper stories. Most field researchers suggest that you never give away rights to the data or control over the final project (Burgess 1991).

The Arrival

Researchers can find themselves in unexpected circumstances upon arrival in the field. When I think about some of the situations that have occurred, I am reminded of the line from one of Hunter S. Thompson's books: "Bad craziness, but it never got weird enough for me." Some of these situations would have been "too weird" for me, and I would probably have retreated hastily. However, many field researchers have persevered despite early days of "bad craziness." Indeed, Rosalie Wax states that smooth early interactions in a setting are not only rare, but suspect (1971:17).

Wax certainly knows from firsthand experience how difficult one's arrival in a setting can be; for the first six weeks that she was at a Japanese-American relocation camp, she felt as if she were losing her mind because no one would talk to her. Other researchers have described themselves as feeling "stupid, clumsy, and less than human" and "full of disorientation, shock, and disequilibrium" during the early days of their research (Wax 1971). Napoleon Chagnon gives the following description of his arrival in the field:

> I looked up and gasped when I saw a dozen burly, naked, filthy, hideous men staring down at us down the shafts of their drawn arrows! Immense wads of green tobacco were stuck between their lower teeth and lips making them look even more hideous, and strands of dark-green slime dripped or hung from their noses. My next discovery was that there were a dozen or so vicious dogs snapping at my legs, circling me as if I were going to be their next meal. I just stood there holding my notebook, helpless and pathetic. (1968:5)

Sometimes the best way to approach the early days in the setting is with a good sense of humor. I try to reassure myself when I'm in an uncomfortable but safe situation that this event will make a wonderful story at a dinner party someday. The need to "put on a happy face" is reflected in some of the writings of researchers who share their early experiences in the field. Wax summarizes how some field researchers recount their early field research experiences:

> Painful and humiliating experiences are easier to talk about if one does not take them too seriously, and it is less distressing to picture oneself as a clown or figure of fun than as a dolt or a neurotic (1971:19).

The purpose of these examples is not to scare you away from field research but to help you appreciate the difficulties of arriving in a setting so that you can be prepared to deal with the potential stresses. Also, I would mislead you if I pretended that the early interactions are simply something to get through so that one can get on with the real business of doing research. It is during this initial period that a fundamental part of field research is being done; everything that follows is affected by these early interactions.

Key Actors

One factor that can help the field researcher move beyond the awkward, and often scary, early days of field research is the assistance of one or more members in the setting. If you can break through, establish rapport, and procure the cooperation of at least one member in the setting, you can usually proceed with the types of interactions and observations necessary for a successful project.

Sometimes it isn't possible to make connections with a member in the setting. For example, Hortense Powdermaker was never able to get involved with anybody she had hoped to study in Hollywood and therefore could not do satisfactory work although she had successfully completed projects in other settings (1966). It took Rosalie Wax over four months before she was able to develop any kind of social relationships among the Japanese-Americans because they assumed she was "a spy for the administration" (1971:18).

Field researchers sometimes refer to the person who rescues and assists them as a **key actor** or **key insider**. A key actor is a member of the setting who is willing to act as a guide and assistant within the setting. Historically, this person has been called an **informant**, but many of us are moving away from this term because of its negative connotations.

Sometimes a key actor is someone the researcher knows prior to doing the research or one of the formal or informal gatekeepers that the researcher got to know while obtaining permission to do the research. Usually, the key insider is someone the researcher met in the early days of the research who is willing to "adopt" the researcher, for often unknown reasons, and become her or his mentor and guide.

Interactions with others in the setting are often easier to establish if the key actor makes introductions. The key actor can help you gain entry, establish rapport, provide explanations, and perform a host of other useful tasks. The key actor may tell you when you have committed a social faux pas or when your life is in danger (Wax 1971). The key insider helps resocialize the field researcher into the ways of the members.

For our project in Midsouth County, Shannon (fictional name) was both our key insider and one of the formal gatekeepers. She was a member of the local Women's Health Coalition in Midsouth County and a public health educator. Several of us also knew her from her days as a graduate student at Virginia Tech. Thus, she provided the link between those of us from the university, the administrators of various health organizations, and the women of Midsouth County who needed health care. Shannon drove us around, introduced us to women at the housing project, and got us access to the dynamic members of grassroots women's organizations; she had access to statistical data for the county and to the Catholic nun who drove the mobile health wagon. Wherever Shannon was welcome, we were welcome.

Although key actors provide a valuable service, there are also costs involved with relying on insiders as your guides. One drawback is that key actors have their own perspectives, biographies, and history that influence what they see, think, and feel are important. The perspective of the insider, while important, may be counter to what most members in the setting feel. Consequently, the insider's perspective should be considered only one of many perspectives and not taken as representative of the group.

Another disadvantage of working with an insider is that it may isolate you from some members of the setting. For example, if you happen to establish rapport with someone who is known in the setting as a total jerk, you might find that others may be unwilling to cooperate with you because of your alliance with this person.

Some textbooks warn beginning researchers not to let the key actor dictate the parameters of the study. While this is basically sound advice, those of us who view field research as a cooperative venture attempt to define the parameters of the study in conjunction with the members in the setting—including the key actor. Consequently, I suggest that the beginning researcher let the parameters of the study emerge from the combined interests of all those involved, paying particular attention in field notes, thoughts, and analyses to the role the key actor had in influencing the outcome of the research.

Informed Consent

In the last chapter I discussed institutional review board approval. Part of the procedure for gaining approval is to have a plan that the board considers ethical for getting informed consent. As always, no set of rules applies to all field settings. For example, if you want to study children, you need to get the children's informed consent as well as the consent of their parents or legal guardians. In some cases, you may need to obtain members' signatures on consent forms. For other settings, particularly public ones, informed consent can be more informal. Those of you planning to do field research should work closely with your class instructor to develop your procedures for informed consent.

Sometimes gaining permission from gatekeepers and obtaining informed consent from members in the setting are the same thing. Remember that both formal and informal gatekeepers can also be members in the setting. Elliot Liebow's work (1994) provides a good example of gaining entry and obtaining informed consent at the same time from the informal gatekeepers.

Liebow volunteered at a soup kitchen and shelter after he retired on disability from 20 years on the job as an anthropologist with the National Institute of Mental Health. Because he thoroughly enjoyed the interactions with the women at the shelter, he decided to do a research project. He first obtained permission from the formal gatekeeper, the shelter director. Because Liebow was already known to the shelter director as a competent and respected volunteer, obtaining permission was as simple as requesting it. However, this was only one level of gatekeeping that he needed to address. He knew that access was also controlled by some of the informal gatekeepers, specifically key shelter residents. He needed to obtain permission from these gatekeepers, and he also needed to obtain informed consent from the rest of the members in the setting.

Gaining permission from these women was fairly easy, but it was not without strings attached. He recounts his experience in the preface of his book:

> "Listen," I said at the dinner table one evening. . . . "I want your permission to take notes. I want to go home at night and write down what I can remember about the things you say and do. Maybe I'll write a book about homeless women." Most of the dozen or so women there nodded their heads or simply shrugged. All except Regina. Her acceptance was conditional. "Only if you promise not to publish before I do," she said. Believing that neither one of us, for different reasons, would ever publish anything in the future, I readily agreed. (1994:ix)

Fortunately, Liebow eventually got Regina's permission to publish. Otherwise, it would have been unethical for him to publish his work because of their agreement.

As noted in Chapter 1, some field researchers engage in covert research in which the members in the setting do not know that they are being observed. Some argue that this is the only way to prevent members from changing their behavior because of the presence of the researcher. However, my goal is to train you in a style of research that is based on honesty and trust. If you can successfully achieve a cooperative relationship with the members, I believe that this more than compensates for what would be lost through reactivity. However, you need to reflect in your field notes and analysis about the impact your presence has in the setting.

Doing research in which all members participate voluntarily through informed consent is easier in theory than in practice. First, informed consent is not static: Once permission is given it can be withdrawn at any time, and the ethical researcher has no choice but to honor the request of a member to no longer participate. Liebow's work provides an example of this. Some women agreed to participate and then withdrew their permission, one extremely late in the process. He writes:

> Originally, I had asked three homeless women and the director of a shelter to write comments on the manuscript. One of the women, after reading a draft of the manuscript, and for reasons not clear to me, angrily decided she did not want to be in the book at all. She did agree to allow herself to be quoted (but not described) in a couple of places. All other references to her were deleted at her request. Similarly, in the second year, one of the more distinctive and more troubled women told me she wanted nothing to do with me or anything I might write. . . . We had gotten along well until the day she saw me in earnest conversation with a woman who had become her enemy. On the theory that "the friend of my enemy is my enemy," she refused to talk to me thereafter (as she had refused to talk to some of the women as well). Also, from that day on, to her I was no longer "Elliot" but "Idiot," as in "Here comes Idiot again to seduce all the women." (1994:xvii)

Another difficulty with informed consent is that it may be impossible to inform everyone who enters a setting that research is in progress. John Van Maanen's work again provides a good illustration of the difficulties and implications of not informing everyone in a setting. All the officers in Van Maanen's study were informed of his role as observer, but their agreement to fully participate was granted only after they felt he passed several tests (not all of which were legal) demonstrating his loyalty and trustworthiness. However, he did not extend informed consent to the citizens he encountered. Since he dressed as a plainclothed police officer, most citizens assumed he was a member of the police force, but "at no time was a citizen ever let in on the partial charade" (1982:113).

It was partly because of his agreements with the police officers that he did not feel compelled to inform the citizens. He argues that once he obtained the consent of the police for him to be a participant observer, then he had an obligation to act as a participant. Thus, Van

Maanen had to "back up" or assist police officers acting in the line of duty. He writes:

> It is also worth noting that the height of moral duplicity would be to create this sort of partnership impression among the people one studies and then refuse to act in line with the implicit bargain such an impression conveys. For me to pose as a friend of the police and then not back them up on a potentially risky adventure, an adventure they may well have undertaken only because of the additional safety they believed my presence provided, would be to violate the very premises of ethnographic research and the importance human relationships play in its enactment. (1982:114)

Most likely the situations you will encounter during your field research will be less extreme. However, even the seemingly most benign setting generates informed consent dilemmas for the researcher. Think about these examples. If you are doing your research in the office of event planning on your campus, certainly you would get informed consent from everyone who works in the office and permission from the proper authorities. However, if the president of the skydiving club comes in to schedule a demonstration jump on your campus commons, do you need to inform him that he is part of your research? If you are doing your research in the financial aid office, do you need to obtain informed consent from the dozens of students that are most likely standing in line at any given moment? If you are doing your research at the laundromat and someone comes in to use the dollar bill changer to get change for a phone call, can you include this activity in your field notes if you have not obtained her permission? As researchers we end up on shaky ground when we start making decisions about when informed consent is important. At the same time, the dynamics of field research are such that the researcher has to make this decision many times during the field research. Some institutional review boards require you to explain your informed consent procedures for both the members of the setting and those who might not be members in the setting but enter it nonetheless.

Relationships

An artist named Ferron sings a song that contains the line "Life don't go clickity-clack along a straight-lined track, it comes together, and it comes apart" (1980). Field research fits Ferron's description.

The life of the field researcher and the lives of those in the setting come together and come apart—not fully merging but not fully independent.

Field research hinges on relationships that ideally are emotional and personal, not formal and hierarchical. Judith Stacey illustrates this in writing about her field study of the daily lives of two families:

> Choosing my next major research project, I was eager for a "hands-on" engagement in the field. Unschooled in fieldwork research as I was, I did not anticipate the depth or the complexity of the emotional experiences I was about to undergo. My heart, much more than my hands, has been engaged with the people portrayed in this book who so generously agreed to subject their family lives to my impertinent sociological scrutiny. (1991:ix)

Those who have written about field research have almost always acknowledged the importance of field relationships. Early textbooks on field research usually have a section on developing rapport with those in the field. The writers of these early texts told us that if we can get along with the members in the setting and establish trust , they will open up and provide us with a wealth of information that we might not have gotten without this rapport. Current advice to field researchers on relationships is more complex than this early view.

As already noted in earlier chapters, trust is not unidirectional. The field researcher is in a reciprocal relationship with the members. Therefore, the onus is on the researcher to be worthy of the trust, respect, and goodwill of those in the setting. Elliot Liebow was keenly aware of the importance of a reciprocal relationship with the homeless women. Several of the women even got to know his daughters. He writes:

> It is difficult to exaggerate the importance of this kind of familiarity. It is essential, I believe, in this kind of study—a participation observer kind of study—that relationships be as symmetrical as possible, that there be a quid pro quo; the women needed to know as much about me as I knew about them. (1994:xii)

Liebow further illustrates how many of us now see members in a setting as collaborators, not as subjects to be conned into cooperating. He continues:

> I think of Betty and Louise and many of the other women as friends. As a friend, I owe them friendship. Perhaps I also owe

them something because I have so much and they have so little, but I do not feel under any special obligation to them as research subjects. Indeed, I do not think of them as "research subjects." Since they knew what I was trying to do and allowed me to do it, they could just as well be considered collaborators in what might fairly be seen as a cooperative enterprise. (1994:xvi)

Gaining **rapport** is an important first step to developing friendships. It would be nice if I could provide a list of things to do to help you achieve rapport. It would be even better if your instructor could just wave a magic wand and have this rapport thing taken care of. Alas, neither is possible. What works in one setting might backfire in another; what works for one of you will not work for others in your class.

Developing rapport requires the same skills that you use in making friends. Unfortunately, it also requires more than that. The members in the setting may be suspicious of your presence; they may be unpleasant to the point of being disgusting; they may use different verbal and nonverbal language than you; they may be incredibly brilliant, beautiful, talented, and well known; and they may range from boring to manic. Your particular configuration of personality styles will also influence your efforts at building rapport. Consequently, it is difficult to give specific directions on building rapport.

Honesty, openness, friendliness, and a willingness to get along are usually good places to start. In time, most people respond to genuine concern and interest in them (Neuman 1991:349). However, remember that gaining rapport is a process that requires constant attention. W. Lawrence Neuman warns us that "rapport is easier to lose once it has been built up than to gain in the first place" (1991: 349). You might want to think about building rapport as tending a delicate pet that requires constant care and feeding.

The status characteristics of all involved affect relationships and rapport in the field in often unpredictable ways. As before, I'll give some examples based on gender, but the principles hold true for race, ethnicity, class, sexual orientation, age, and the intersection of these characteristics.

Carol A. B. Warren is a superb field researcher who has written an excellent book on gender issues involved in field research (1988). She provides some wonderful examples in her book that illustrate the complex ways in which gender affects field research relationships. I summarize several of her illustrations below, but I encourage the interested student to read her book for more details.

Norris Johnson (1986) had initial trouble forming good field relationships with women teachers during his study of elementary
schools in the midwestern United States. The women teachers were
used to, but resentful of, the intrusion of men into their area. The
male janitorial staff and male supervisors frequently entered their
classrooms unannounced, without knocking, and without their permission. Johnson was able to gain the respect of the women teachers
by avoiding flirting, by deferring to their authority and territory, and
by acting unlike other males in this setting.

Being a woman doesn't necessarily make things easier. In some
settings, the "hypervisibility" of women can negatively interfere
with field relationships if the women get labeled as spies. Jennifer
Hunt (1984) encountered this problem when she attempted to do
field research on an urban police department while the department
was in the middle of a lawsuit for gender discrimination against female officers.

In contrast, Warren (1988) notes that her "invisibility as a
woman" in some settings resulted in relationships and access to locations that would have been denied a man. She reports that men in
a drug rehabilitation center talked to her freely and allowed her to
roam in areas off-limits to outsiders because they viewed her as "just
a broad" and therefore harmless. In another setting, no one ques-
tioned her access to file drawers because of the presumption that she
was a secretary or file clerk (1982); the same assumption may not
have been made if she were a man.

In summary, since gender is such a key organizing device in virtually all settings, male and female researchers will be treated differently by those in the setting. Because gender has a bearing on the
nature of relationships and interactions, men and women will come
to know different aspects of the cultures they investigate (Warren
1988:5).

Other features of one's biography also affect the research process.
One's physical attractiveness, neatness habits, standards of time,
communication skills, physical health, table manners, hair color and
style, level of expertise, and musical taste and abilities are just a few
of the many potential factors that affect field relationships in complex and often unknown ways. Liebow shared with his readers some
of his characteristics that he thinks might have made a difference in
his interactions with the homeless women. He writes:

> It is difficult to be precise about how I was perceived by the
> women. I am 6'1" and weigh about 175 pounds. I had a lot of

white hair but was otherwise nondescript. I dressed casually, often in corduroy pants, shirt, and cardigan. The fact that I was Jewish did not seem to matter much one way or another so far as I could tell. . . . Most of the women probably liked having me around. Male companionship was generally in short supply and the women often made a fuss about the few male volunteers. . . . The fact that I had written a book that was available at the library (three or four women took the trouble to read it) enhanced my legitimacy in their eyes. (1994:x)

In this next example, religious beliefs seem to be at the center of the interactions, but we still are not able to precisely specify the dynamics at work. Judith Stacey (1991) studied two families during her field experience, and one family member, Pam, was a deeply religious person. After reading parts of Stacey's report, Pam was upset by the "instrumental account" Stacey had given in the manuscript of Pam's reborn religious faith.

What might account for the disjuncture between how Stacey wrote about Pam's religion and the way Pam views her religion? Let's list some possibilities.

1. Maybe Stacey sees her own religion in an instrumental light so she subsequently projects that onto how Pam sees hers.

2. Maybe there wasn't sufficient rapport between the two women for Stacey to gain an adequate understanding of Pam's religious beliefs. For example, maybe the two of them are from different social classes and had trouble communicating with each other.

3. Maybe Pam's presentation of her religion was affected by her perception of Stacey's religious beliefs. For example, if Pam didn't think Stacey would appreciate the more spiritual side of her religion, she may have emphasized those things about her religion that she did think Stacey could relate to. Pam did know that Stacey was not at all religious.

4. Maybe Pam was trying to convert Stacey so she emphasized the practical benefits of her religion.

I suspect that all four factors and more contributed to the gap between Stacey's and Pam's perceptions.

The dynamics between the two may have been something like this. Pam has feelings about her religion that affect what she relates to Stacey. Pam has perceptions about Stacey's religious beliefs—and these are filtered through Pam's own feelings about religion. Because of Pam's perception of Stacey's beliefs, Pam modifies her accounts of her religion. Stacey has feelings about her own religion (or lack thereof) that affect her understanding of Pam's religious accounts. Stacey presents her interpretation of the modified account in her book.

At this point, you might feel it would have been a whole lot easier for Stacey to ask Pam to respond to a survey question on religiosity! However, such a question would be inaccurate for understanding Pam's religion within the context of her everyday life. The beauty of field research is that you can at least start to address some of the complexity of how people make sense out of the world in relationship to others in it.

The previous example partially illustrates how what is drawn from a setting is affected by the researcher's own biography. A researcher's own history, personality, belief system, and so on will affect what the researcher considers important enough to note. Additionally, the members' perceptions of the researcher's characteristics will affect how the members present themselves. These mechanisms are fluid and change over time, sometimes leading to more trust and understanding and other times not. Relationships that were relatively open can occasionally erode as the researcher and the members gain insights about each other.

In sum, although the goal of field research is to understand the everyday life of those in the setting, this understanding is a negotiated process, affected by the interactions between the researcher and the members. The status characteristics and other personal characteristics of all involved influence the nature of the interactions. The inevitable personal and emotional reactions among the researcher and the members in the setting shape the character of the transactions and their interpretations (Emerson 1988:176). As stated by Emerson:

> Once some sort of relation has been created, the character of that particular relationship determines what sorts of experiences and hence what kinds of experiential and intuitive insights the fieldworker will gain. (1988:176)

Experiences, interactions, and relationships are the sources of data for the field researcher. The researcher engages in "active, empathetic participation in the rounds and structures of life and meaning of those" in the setting as a means of data collection (Emerson 1988:15).

This immersion in the setting leads to the distinctive field research mode of understanding. As stated by Emerson, "interpretive understanding is acquired through regular and intimate involvement, maintained over time and under a variety of diverse circumstances, in the worlds of others" (Emerson 1988:15). One way that field researchers immerse themselves in the setting is through careful observations.

Observations

When most of us think of observing, we tend to think of observing with our eyes. Watching is certainly an important part of collecting data in the field setting; however, so are listening, smelling, touching, and tasting. Sometimes in the social sciences we forget the importance of using all our senses. It is not at all likely that a survey researcher would tell his or her readers that the people who took the survey smelled bad. In contrast, multiple sensory input is common in the hard sciences. Medical doctors, for example, use the sense of smell as one of their diagnostic tools. Consequently, when I talk about observing, please remember that I mean doing so by using all the senses.

Observations of Physical Surroundings

Visiting the home of a new acquaintance can quickly tell you a lot about the person. You usually can tell if the person is a music fan, is a sports devotee, is well traveled, or likes to cook. Is the person neat or cluttered? A 35-inch home theater in the center of the room says something different about the person's television viewing patterns than would a 19-inch television tucked away in the corner. Our physical surroundings reflect a great deal about who we are.

Not surprisingly, field researchers pay attention to physical surroundings. However, it is the social implications of the physical surroundings that are important to the field researcher. It would be singularly uninteresting for me to tell you that I know a room on your campus that is 12 feet by 13 feet. The room dimensions become meaningful only when we understand the social significance of this amount of space. For example, space is often used as an indicator of social status. A room this size might be a sign of high social status if it were the office of the athletic director, but the size might indicate the low prestige of the theater department if this were the only room on campus allocated to the entire department. Consequently, when field researchers observe physical surroundings, they hope to understand the implications of the physical surroundings for the social world.

When you begin to observe a setting, you might start by noting the *lighting*. Lighting conveys a great deal of social meaning. Think, for example, of how a flick of the lights indicates that the intermission is over during a theater production. Is the lighting soft and subdued, bright and cold, inadequate, or designed to draw attention to or from something? What kind of atmosphere does the lighting convey? Does it affect how individuals in the setting interact with each other?

Color is also used to create a mood, so the colors used in the setting should be documented. Are there neutral colors or do the colors tend toward bold? Are the colors soft and soothing? Are the colors well coordinated or do they seem haphazard? What purpose might they serve? Do the colors make you feel safe or anxious?

The *smell* of the setting is important too. Does it smell clean even though it might not look it, or vice versa? Are there scents and perfumes? Does it smell new or old? Can you smell the presence of pets, children, food, leather, oil, laundry, or chemicals? Does it have the scent of romance, family, or business? Report smells early in your entry to the setting. Your later reaction to the smells will probably be less profound because we adjust to smells. In some settings, your sense of smell may become more acute with time.

Take note of the background *sounds*. Is the space full of laughter, sounds of machinery, piped-in music, telephones, or silence? How are changes in sounds tolerated; do people react quickly to changes or are they ignored? Are sounds used to summon individuals and convey information? An example of this is the tones used on airplanes to discreetly signal flight attendants. Like our sense of smell, our ability to hear sounds changes with exposure. Therefore, document background sounds throughout your stay in a setting.

Also pay close attention to the *objects* in the space: plants, furniture, books, tools, storage units, and so forth. Are the objects primarily functional or decorative? Are they in good or poor condition? Do some objects make political statements? What do the objects indicate about status? What atmosphere do they seem to convey? For example, consider the difference between a sign in a business that says "The customer is always right" and one that says "We reserve the right to refuse service to anyone."

Weather and *temperature* are part of the physical surroundings. Pay particular attention to the relationships between weather and moods and behaviors. Are there more or fewer people on the street when it is hot? What rituals are used to deal with extremes in temperature?

Record your observations and your responses to them to help in getting at the social significance of the physical surroundings. More importantly, seek out how those in the setting perceive the social implications of the physical surroundings. You need to understand the meanings they attach to their surroundings, not just the meaning you attach.

One of my students had an experience during her field research that illustrates this point effectively. Nicole began her field research at a local home for old people by observing the colors used in the building. Much to her surprise, the decor had lots of bright colors, such as red, black, and orange—colors that seemed almost gaudy to her. She was expecting teal, soft blue, and mauve. She reported in her field notes that she didn't like the color choices. They made her feel jumpy. However, after she spent some time there she learned that as we age our eyes are less able to distinguish among softer colors. The colors needed to be strong to enable most residents of the home to see and enjoy them. The home had recently been redecorated by a designer who specialized in designs for geriatric centers. The elderly residents, Nicole found out, were quite pleased with the changes in color scheme. When asked about the colors, one of the residents said, "Oh yes, they make me feel so much happier than before." Nicole avoided a mistake in her field research by not limiting her interpretations of the colors to only her reactions to them.

Observations of Members

You will spend most of your time as a field researcher observing the people in the setting. A good place to begin is to notice the status characteristics of those in the setting. On the surface, this sounds like a relatively easy task: You note the gender, race, and approximate age of the people being observed. However, do not let your personal experiences deceive you. For example, just because you are used to thinking of welders as men, do not assume that the person behind the welder's mask is a man without further information. When I first visited Nicaragua I consistently estimated children's ages as much younger than they were and adult ages as much older than they were. The poverty of the people had a great effect on the physical signs we often use to estimate age, such as height. In some settings small distinctions in skin color are important while in others major differences are ignored. Consequently, your description of a particular individual's race may change over time as you learn the racial code used in the setting.

The observation of an individual's appearance is not limited to status characteristics. Nearly every feature of the individual is important. Height and weight make a difference in interactions and so should be noted. For example, do tall college men have a social advantage over short college men? Certainly, we know that physical attractiveness affects all sorts of interactions. However, because what is considered physically attractive varies from setting to setting, field researchers need to avoid relying solely on their own standards of attractiveness. Remember Napoleon Chagnon's description of the "hideous men" with tobacco wads between their lips and "dark-green slime" dripping from their noses (Chagnon 1968:5)? Chagnon was absolutely correct to record his perception of the men's attractiveness since this certainly affected his interactions with them. However, at this point we have no idea if his perceptions were consistent with the perceptions of those in the setting. It could very well be the case that many in the setting found these men highly desirable.

Dress and hairstyle also convey meaning. You know the code for your own setting, but you will have to learn a new code for most settings you observe. Are mohawk haircuts and nose rings considered radical or normative on your campus? Are they normative or radical among Wall Street brokers or among a group of artists living in Soho? Wearing a bandanna may hold little meaning for you but may be highly significant for some gang members. Do the number, location, and size of earrings have meaning in the setting you are observing? Make sure that you record styles and patterns even if you aren't sure if they have any social significance. As you learn more about a setting, you might be pleased that you wisely recorded details that at the time had little meaning for you.

Observations of Nonverbal and Verbal Behaviors

Most observations are of behaviors—such things as who comes, who goes, who does what with whom, when, and how, routine activities, traffic patterns, special events, random behaviors, and unanticipated happenings. While writing a descriptive account of behaviors is fairly easy, the goal of field research is to understand, not merely describe. Again, immersion in the field setting gives a researcher the best chance of assessing the meanings behind behaviors.

One thing that can help your understanding is paying close attention to *body language,* an extremely important part of communication. What facial expressions are used in what situations? How are people standing in relationship to each other? What is their posture? How much space do they take up—expansive or small relative to their size? How do they move—do they appear confident or unsure? How much eye contact is there and for how long? Who is touching whom in what context? Does the body language change as individuals enter and leave a setting or does it vary by the status characteristics of the participants?

Verbal behaviors are another major category of observations. Field researchers often record the text of conversations verbatim to retain the voices of the speakers. However, field researchers are also aware that talk is not objective reporting of factual data. Rather, talk also is part of, and not independent of, the social world. So the field researcher explores the way verbal accounts are used to create social meaning within the context of social relationships (Emerson 1988). More is said about the importance of talk in the section on interviewing.

To help locate the talk within the larger setting, pay attention to the *characteristics of the speech and the speakers.* What types of words are being used during the conversations? For example, are slang words, cuss words, or technical words used regularly? Does the setting have an argot (words and meanings specific to that setting)? What do these things tell us about the meaning of the speech and the setting?

Observe who does most of the talking and whose suggestions are followed as well as whose are rejected or ignored. For example, children may talk to parents more than parents talk to children in a grocery store, but in most cases, what is said by the parents carries more influence. Who interrupts and who doesn't is worthy of note. What do these behaviors tell you about power and status rankings in this setting?

You can gather hints of embedded meaning by listening to the tone of a conversation: polite, hostile, relaxed, instrumental, playful, or formal. Are voices soft or loud, modulated or monotone? Remember that how something is said is frequently more important than what is said.

A mistake that field researchers sometimes make when observing is that they act like a voice-activated tape recorder or a light fixture that turns on when it senses movement. When someone speaks or moves, the field researcher starts writing down text, observing body language, and so forth. When the action stops, the field researcher takes a break and waits for someone in the setting to throw the on switch. Even when nothing seems to be happening, the field researcher needs to be aware and analytical. For example, in a study of a suburban community, it is as important to note who is not working in their yards on a Saturday morning as it is to note who is.

The importance of actively observing the nonaction is probably not new to you. You may have been trained in art classes to look at the negative spaces formed by the objects in addition to the objects themselves; or you may have heard the saying "not making a decision is making a decision." However, many of us are used to only subconsciously noticing the background while consciously reacting to the foreground. In fact, in many settings the background is purposely hidden. During a play, for example, lighting changes are supposed to help create mood changes, but the audience is supposed to notice only the change in the mood—not the lighting. As field researchers we need to fight the tendency to observe only the foreground; we need to observe both background and foreground and how they work together. Otherwise, we run the risk of paying attention only to the high-status members because in most settings not all group members have equal access to center stage. Field researchers are well aware that much of the important work in a setting is done by those in the background.

When you are observing, do so ethically. Do not sneak into areas off-limits to outsiders or wander into places where you haven't been granted permission. If you have been given permission to be in a particular space, this does not mean you have free license to observe everything there. For example, if you are observing the secretarial staff in a department, this does not mean it is OK for you to go through desk drawers or search through computer files without explicit permission. Doing field research is not a justification for observing private behaviors, places, or things without explicit permission.

At the start of your research, you have the almost overwhelming task of observing everything. It is dangerous to assume that one knows what is important to observe and what can be ignored. However, as your research progresses, as your understanding grows, and as your goals become more specific, your observations will become more focused. Decisions about what to observe are part of the researcher's daily reflective process, and these decisions are affected by the social relationships in which the researcher takes part.

David Fetterman (1989) observed some bad smells by Western standards during his research. Fortunately, as a skilled field researcher, he was more concerned with good field relations than he was with Western hygiene. Here is part of his tale:

> During my stay with the Bedouins, I tried not to let my bias for Western hygiene practices and monogamy surface in my interactions or writings. I say *tried* because my reaction to one of my first acquaintances, a Bedouin with a leathery face and feet, was far from neutral. I was astonished. I admired his ability to survive and adapt in a harsh environment, moving from one water hole to the next throughout the desert. However, my personal reaction to the odor of his garments (particularly after a camel ride) was far from impartial. He shared his jacket with me to protect me from the heat. I thanked him, of course, because I appreciated the gesture and did not want to insult him. But I smelled like a camel for the rest of the day in the dry desert heat. I thought I didn't need the jacket because we were only a kilometer or two from our destination, Saint Catherine's monastery, but the short trip took forever—up rocky paths and down through *wadis* or valleys. I learned later that without his jacket I would have suffered from sunstroke. The desert heat is so dry that perspiration evaporates almost immediately, and an inexperienced traveler does not always notice when the temperature climbs above 130 degrees Fahrenheit. By slowing down the evaporation rate, the jacket helped me retain water. Had I rejected his jacket and, by implication, Bedouin hygiene practices, I would have baked, and I would never have understood how much their lives revolve around water, the desert's most precious resource. Our seemingly circuitous ride followed a hidden water route, not a straight line to the monastery. (1989:33)

You will probably not find yourself in as precarious a position as Fetterman if you do field research for a class assignment. However, the first point of this example is to illustrate how smell was part of Fetterman's observations. More importantly, I also use this dramatic example to reinforce the point that the concern for social relationships lies at the heart of field research. Regardless of what one is observing, the social relationship is primary. Not only did Fetterman's concern for the relationship with the Bedouin lead to a better understanding of desert culture, it literally saved his life.

Informal Interviews

In addition to using all the senses when observing, field researchers spend a great deal of time conversing with the members in the setting. One particular type of interaction that is valuable to the field researcher is the informal interview. An **informal interview** is a conscious attempt by the researcher to find out more information about the setting and the person.

You may have already learned about structured interviews. Therefore, it might be useful to contrast the informal interview with structured interviews. Structured interviews are usually scheduled in advance, are expected to take a specific amount of time, and consist of a list of questions prepared in advance and asked of all those being interviewed. The interviewer controls the order and pace of the questions and tries to keep the respondent on track.

Training of interviewers usually includes a series of don'ts. For example:

- Don't deviate from the standard explanation of the study.
- Don't deviate from the sequence of questions or question wording.
- Don't let the subject interrupt the interview.
- Don't let other people interject anything into the interview.
- Don't give the subject any of your personal views.
- Don't interpret the meaning of a question or give clarifications that are not provided in training by your supervisor.
- Don't improvise by adding answer categories or making word changes (Fontana and Frey 1994:362).

I remember being trained in graduate school on ways to avoid answering questions when giving a structured interview. We were taught to say things such as "I'm here to learn your opinion, not to give mine" when subjects asked us something.

In contrast, the informal interview is reciprocal—both the researcher and the member in the setting engage in the dialogue. Field researchers ask questions, but they also answer them. Both researcher and member share feelings, impressions, ideals, and information. The informal interview often goes where it wants to go and is affected by the context in which it is taking place.

The informal interview does not have a set number of questions or time allocated for each interview. The field researcher can ask one member one question and ask another person many questions. Informal interviews can last a few minutes or hours, and rarely is this known in advance. While informal interviews can be scheduled by the field researcher, they most often take place spontaneously.

In field research, interviews are not equally distributed: some members might be interviewed many times, others only once or a few times, and some members not at all. Sometimes an informal interview begins between the field researcher and a member and then other members join in. The interview may continue long after the original member has left the setting. Informal interviews are not about structure and hierarchy but about talking and mutual discovery (Neuman 1991:367).

While this notion of mutual discovery sounds great, most of your interviews or conversations will not consist of analytical insights and profound truths. Mostly they will be about fairly routine, mundane sorts of things. Sometimes conversations won't make sense. One cannot always be sure why that is the case. Maybe we missed the point because we were not paying attention or we don't know the argot being used; maybe the speaker communicated the point badly; or maybe the speaker isn't sure what the point of the talk is. Members in a setting are often unsure, equivocal, ambiguous, confused, and unaware of how, when, where, and why things are happening. John Van Maanen warns us that it is fairly routine for conversations to be obscured in some "existential fog" (1982:141). Nonetheless, most of one's field notes will be made up of trying to make sense out of the talk in the setting.

The questions you ask will depend upon the research setting and the reciprocal relationship you have established with the members in the setting. All I want to do here is give a few general suggestions and reassure you that it is perfectly acceptable for the field researcher to ask "stupid questions" in the beginning stages of research (Fetterman 1989).

When you first start doing informal interviews, you may try "grand tour questions" (Fetterman 1989). A grand tour question is one that you hope will be answered with a broad overview of the setting. For example, one of the first things you might ask of someone in a setting is whether they would mind showing you around. If they are inclined to do so, you can start to learn where things are, what things are called, and what is important—at least to the person giving the tour. For example, our request to be shown around in Midsouth County got us an automobile trip around the county. Our "tour guide" drove by and pointed out all the churches in the county without us specifically asking her to do so. Although this might have meant that religion was important only to our guide, the fact that there were so many churches and they were so well cared for told us that religion was probably important to many people in Midsouth.

Many of your early questions will be requests for general information, such as "What goes on in this part of the building?" "Who are those people over there?" "What is that used for?" "How is that done?" As you gain insights from these general questions, you can start to ask more specific ones, which can then lead to important insights into the setting.

I'll use another example from Midsouth to illustrate this point. Early in our stay, we asked about the locations of various buildings and services. We were told that the grocery store was in one part of town, the health center in an entirely different part of town, and the hospital in yet another part. None of these buildings was particularly close to a large housing project. We learned from this that we needed to ask specific questions about transportation in our interviews because these services were clearly not within walking distance of each other. We asked questions such as "How do you get to the health clinic?" "Do you have a car you can drive?" "How good are the buses for getting you to the health clinic?" "Do you ever have any trouble getting your husband to drive you to the clinic?" and "Do you ever take a taxi to the health clinic?"

As a result of these questions, we learned that many of the women did not have cars, but Medicaid would pay for a taxi to take them to get health care. This led us to talk with some of the taxi drivers. One local taxi driver explained to my colleague that she did not earn much from driving women to the local health clinic. She said that some taxi drivers encouraged the women to go to hospitals and clinics in another county so that the driver could earn more money. This caused delays in health care, underutilization of local services, and increased costs to taxpayers. The taxi drivers were able to persuade the women to go to another county by perpetuating the rumor that the local health services were not as good as those available in other counties. This rumor led to mistrust and avoidance of local services, sometimes resulting in women getting no care or more expensive care elsewhere. Before going to Midsouth, I would not have guessed that the reputation of a health clinic was affected by the dependence upon Medicaid-reimbursed travel.

We could not have learned about this problem if my colleague had not developed sufficient rapport with the woman she interviewed. The trusting relationship between my colleague and the taxi driver was at the foundation of this insight; asking the question in an appropriate manner was only secondary.

The conversation with the taxi driver is a success story. Unfortunately, as field researchers, we probably have more interviews that don't even get off the ground than we do successful ones. Van Maanen relates this response to his attempts to talk with a police officer in the field:

> I don't have nothing to say to you and you don't have nothing to say to me. I'm putting in my time. I've got a year to go until I pull the pin and I don't want any trouble. I don't know what you want and I wouldn't give a s____ even if I did. You mind your business and I'll mind mine. (1982:111)

This was one of his friendlier rejections. Field researchers need to be prepared for these sorts of rejections and respect people's wishes not to be interviewed.

I hesitate to give a series of techniques for effective interviewing such as is sometimes included in textbooks. For example, some authors list rules about what is and what is not an acceptable question such as, "Do not ask 'why' questions because they are difficult to answer and sometimes put the person answering on the defensive." In contrast to the rule approach, I agree with Fontana and Frey that interviews are more like "real conversations," "give and take," and "empathic understanding" than a series of rules to follow. They write that this approach to interviewing is

> more honest, morally sound, and reliable, because it treats the respondent as an equal, allows him or her to express personal feelings, and therefore presents a more "realistic" picture than can be uncovered using traditional interview methods. (1994: 371)

In fact, there is some concern that the focus on techniques and tactics of interviewing are really ways of manipulating respondents and thus may be unethical (Oakley 1981; Fontana and Frey 1994). Maurice Punch (1986) suggests that, as interviewers, our first concern should be to exercise moral responsibility. I interpret his comment to mean that we have to be extremely careful that our interviews are ethical.

We have already discussed the ethical issues of informed consent, avoiding harm, and covert research—all of which are relevant to the interviewing process. There is no need to repeat them here other than to reiterate that tape-recording interviews without explicit permission is unethical. It is not enough to inform a member that you are going to tape-record and let them protest if they have a problem with that. You need to explain why you want to record the interview and then ask for their permission.

An additional ethical concern is to be sensitive to the context in which an informal interview takes place. Being sensitive to the context means focusing on more than whether one is going to get an honest answer in the setting. What might be an ethical question in one setting might be unethical in another. For example, I wouldn't ask a teenager in front of her parents if she ever had an abortion. Her parents may assume that the fact that I asked the question implied I had some information as to whether their daughter was sexually active. She may be in trouble for this long after I've left the scene. Consequently, asking her in front of her parents can potentially cause her harm—regardless of her sexual activity or her honesty in answering. Thus, I would consider the question unethical in that setting but possibly acceptable in another setting.

It is not enough, however, to make sure that you ask sensitive questions in private. I believe that people have a right to their privacy and research goals do not give researchers the right to ask anything they want. It is not appropriate for researchers to probe for secret gossip or some personally painful detail. "Getting the dirt" on someone is not a goal of field research.

It is not necessarily unethical for researchers to ask for personal information or for a member to disclose such information under the right circumstances. However, be careful with personal topics so as not to cause the members any harm, including emotional distress. Watch body language and other nonverbal clues closely because these may give you a hint that you are on dangerous ground during a conversation. If you notice signs of distress, back off that particular line of conversation. Unfortunately, you often don't know what someone considers a painful or sensitive issue until it is too late. I remember doing an interview with a college student that included questions on family violence and disordered eating. The interview had lasted about an hour and had gone smoothly right up to the point where I asked her how many sisters she had. She broke into tears and cried for several minutes before regaining composure. Although in this case she reassured me that all she needed was a few tissues, I gave her the number of the campus counseling center, my home number, and the number for a 24-hour hot line in case she wanted to talk later. As a field researcher, you need to be prepared for the unexpected.

During interviews, field researchers need to be good listeners, but we also have to be careful not to promise, even if only implicitly, more than we can deliver. For example, most of us do not have the skills to be counselors, and we should avoid taking on that role (Fetterman 1989). We need to think about the ethical implications of helping people explore problems (for example, family violence) while we are collecting data in the field and then leaving them without support once our research is completed.

Along with our emphasis on ethical interviewing, field researchers are increasingly concerned about the effects of status characteristics on the interview process. This was not always the case. The traditional literature took the position that if the interviewer was objective and neutral and used the proper demeanor to get the subject to talk freely, then any effect of status characteristics would be rendered moot.

Given the importance of status characteristics in all other aspects of field research, it should be obvious that they affect interviews. Indeed, a growing body of literature now explores the complexity of status characteristics and the interview process. For example, we know that female interviewers more frequently than male interviewers have to face sexual overtures, sexual harassment, or being treated as lower in status during interviews. These factors impact the interview. We also know that the race of the interviewer and the respondent affects the dynamics of an interview. The importance of race and ethnicity can be illustrated by the debate within academic literature on whether women need to be of the same race and ethnicity for an interview between two women to be effective.

Although this and other debates will no doubt continue for a long time, most scholars who write about the effects of status characteristics suggest that greater reciprocity in the interview process is the best way to deal with the impact of status characteristics. Fontana and Frey write:

> Thus the emphasis is shifting to allow the development of a closer relation between interviewer and respondent, attempting to minimize status differences and doing away with the traditional hierarchical situation in interviewing. Interviewers can show their human side and answer questions and express feelings. Methodologically, this new approach provides a greater

spectrum of responses and a greater insight into respondents—
or "participants," to avoid the hierarchical pitfall. (1994:370)

If we can close the distance during interviews, we might have a better chance of understanding each other when we talk. This is just another illustration of the importance of good field relationships.

Understanding each other is not the same thing, of course, as getting at the truth. Remember from Chapter 2 that field researchers
usually start from the assumption that there is no objective reality.
Even if you believe that there is an objective reality, you probably accept that different people have different interpretations of this reality.

Multiple viewpoints or realities are not a problem for the field researcher. One of the strengths of field research is that diversities and
similarities can be recognized and possibly even understood. As a
field researcher you will not go about trying to figure out who is
right and who is wrong. Interview data will be contradictory and influenced by us as researchers. Lots of reflectivity and honesty in the
analysis and reporting of the data is the best that we can hope for at
this stage.

Multiple Methods

Field researchers sometimes supplement interactions, observations,
and interviews with techniques used more commonly in other methods during their research. For example, some researchers supplement informal interviews with structured interviews. Life or oral
histories are another, and extremely time-consuming, form of interview sometimes used. The researcher gathers oral histories by having the person recall events from the past. Focus groups are popular
among some field researchers. These consist of asking a fairly homo-
geneous group of approximately 7 to 10 participants a series of
open-ended questions. During focus groups, the researcher uses
probes to gain clarification of answers and to get further information. Another common data collection technique used by field researchers is analysis of documents—newspapers, fliers, grade
sheets, interoffice memos, song lyrics, and so on. The world of tech-
nology has entered field research through the use of videotape and
photographs. More and more field researchers supplement their
field work experiences with self-reported survey data. The following
two examples from current literature illustrate how researchers combine other techniques of data collection with field research.

Linda Blum and Elizabeth Vandewater (1993) were interested in changing definitions of masculinity from the point of view of white, middle-class, married women. The social group they studied contained members of La Leche League—an organization dedicated to breastfeeding and mother primacy. Blum and Vandewater describe their methods as follows:

> This study is based on three sources of qualitative data, reflecting the multiple levels of League discourse and our dual research questions. (1) The first author conducted participant observation fieldwork, attending repeated meetings of three local groups, to examine how the League ideology was employed by leaders and participants in group settings. The local groups drew from affluent and working-class areas. (2) The first author also conducted 24 in-depth interviews with participants, particularly scrutinizing how individuals' views might vary from the organization's stance. Twenty respondents were drawn from volunteers at the local meetings, with an additional four recommended. Of the 24, 9 were leaders and 15 were nonleaders. The tape-recorded interviews took place in the respondents' homes, averaging two hours. (3) Finally, both authors analyzed League publications representing the organization's formal ideology. This was supplemented by participant observation attendance at a statewide conference, as well as several informational phone conversations made to the national headquarters. (1993:5–6)

Mindy Stombler and Patricia Yancey Martin also took a multi-method approach in their study of fraternity "little sister" organizations. Stombler conducted participant observations at one fraternity, "including observation of little sister rush, several parties and social events, and an orientation meeting of newly chosen little sisters" (1994:154). Both researchers held open-ended, in-depth interviews with 17 women who were little sisters from seven men's social fraternities, the president of an Interfraternity Council who had led a drive to disband little sister organizations, two little sister coordinators who were fraternity brothers, one fraternity president, the head of a Greek Affairs Task Force that recommended disbanding little sister organizations, and eight university officials. Finally, they examined official inquiry and commission reports, local and national fraternity and sorority publications, and newspaper and televised reports of sexual assaults on fraternity little sisters (1994:154–155).

There isn't space in this guide to provide instructions on how to use the wide variety of different techniques that supplement field research, and numerous well-written books can help you learn about these other techniques. However, if you decide to supplement your field research by using some of these other techniques in the field, you should be careful to do so in a way that does not violate the overall philosophy of field research. For example, it is inappropriate to create a trusting reciprocal relationship with a member and then treat him or her as a subject during a structured interview.

Using other methods to supplement standard data collection in field research is optional. Most researchers, however, view the taking of field notes as essential to the field research process.

Field Notes

John and Lyn Lofland write the following about **field notes**:

> Aside from getting along in the setting, the fundamental concrete task of the observer is the taking of field notes. If you are not doing so, you might as well not be in the setting. (1984:72)

I rely heavily on the work of the Loflands in the discussion that follows. The interested reader is encouraged to turn to the original sources for more details about field notes and field research in general.

Field notes are the backbone of collecting and analyzing field data. An oversimplified view of field notes is that they are the means by which the field researcher jots down observations in order not to forget them later. However, field notes are much more than a memory tool. Their creation is part of the analytic process.

The first component of field notes consists of *mental notes*. As you interact in the setting, you make mental notes of your experiences. Train yourself to remember observations—such as who was there, what was said, who left first, and how you felt when the person left. As a field researcher, you will be bombarded with massive amounts of detail, and you'll forget large amounts of this input fairly quickly. However, you have a better chance of remembering if you consciously and actively take mental notes of what you want to remember.

Jotted notes constitute the second component of field notes. One type of jotted note is a memory cue for a mental note. You might write "invisible walls" to remind yourself to write later in detail how displaced flood victims in a school gymnasium found ways to create "walls" around their cots to give the illusion that they had some private space. Key phrases, counts, quotes, and easily forgotten details should be jotted down.

Jotted notes can contain thoughts and observations previously forgotten and then recovered. For example, if some observation today triggers something that you forgot to write down yesterday, quickly jot a note about it. Jotted notes also provide memory cues for things you want to pursue later. For example, you may make a quick note to yourself to ask the head lifeguard a particular question the next time she is at the pool. Ideas, feelings, brilliant conclusions, and things that you want to ponder should be jotted down. Don't censor yourself.

The phrase "never leave home without it" may refer to a credit card, but it also refers to a small tablet or notebook in which the field researcher jots notes. I always take several with me, although I usually carry only one at a time, and I make sure that there is always at least one pen attached to the pages. In lieu of a notebook, napkins, matchbook covers, and sales receipts will do. Maybe some of you have already found creative surfaces for exchanging phone numbers. I have even written notes on the back of my hand rather than risk forgetting. However, a tablet carried for this purpose is best.

Although you don't have to hide your jotted notes during overt research, making a big production of note taking can be disconcerting to the members. It is usually best to jot them quickly and then add more details at inconspicuous moments. An exception to this is during interviews; sometimes members expect you to take notes—otherwise they might think you are not really interested in what they are saying.

Lofland and Lofland also have a category that they call "fuller jottings" (1984). They suggest that as you wait for a bus, ride the elevator, stand in line, rest your feet, and even use the bathroom, you elaborate on your earlier jottings.

The jotted notes and mental notes are the basis for full field notes. I will first present some of the types of material contained in full field notes and then discuss the practical aspect of creating field notes.

Following a similar system as the jotted notes, Lofland (1971) lists five types of material that typically appear in field notes. The first is a *chronological log* or running description of your observations and interactions throughout the period in the field. Observations of physical surroundings, people, behaviors, and conversations should be written up in detail. Make sure that you date each set of field notes and include exact or approximate times of occurrence. Once a person or surrounding is described in the field notes, you do not have to repeat these for the next day's field notes unless something has changed (Lofland and Lofland 1984).

The running description should be concrete. Focus as best you can on what Lofland calls the "raw behavior"; do not attempt at this point to explain why someone did something or to guess how they felt when they were doing so. Make sure that you keep clear distinctions between something you saw or thought and what members in the setting saw and thought (Lofland 1971). For example, if Eve told you that Sandy bought her a new pottery kiln because he was happy with their relationship, make sure you write down that this is Eve's interpretation of Sandy's behavior—not necessarily yours or Sandy's.

Many researchers keep their accounts of conversations and informal interviews in this section, although some researchers who do more structured interviews keep a set of interview notes separate from their field notes. You should develop a system to differentiate in your notes among verbatim quotes, close paraphrases, and general recall. You might put double quotation marks around verbatim material, single quotation marks around paraphrasing, and no quotation marks when you think you have captured the gist of someone's statement but are not using his or her words.

Many field researchers supplement the running description with visual aids—maps, diagrams, drawings, and photographs. Often you can collect some observed objects, such as programs, newspaper articles, menus, and brochures. These can be included with the field notes.

A second category of material in the field notes includes *things previously forgotten* and now recalled. Some of these you will get from your jotted notes. Others will appear as part of the process of writing your field notes. Something that had previously seemed insignificant might on this day seem worthy of note, possibly because a similar event or item appeared again. Include it with this day's notes, but try your best to document the time, date, and context of when it was first experienced.

The third type of material in the field notes consists of the *analytic ideas and inferences* that you start to have. You might have some ideas about the social meanings of particular events or notice patterns that seem to fit a conceptual category. Write down your interpretations of interactions. Are themes that you want to explore starting to emerge? If so, write them down. Think routinely about the goals of your study and write down any potential insights you have about them. Ideas that seem trivial, obvious, and far-fetched are all acceptable. Put them all—good, bad, and unsure—in the field notes.

The process of creating complete field notes is part of your analysis. You do not wait until after you have left the field and returned to your apartment to start your data analysis. Analysis of the data is an ongoing project and occurs while you are engaging in interactions and writing field notes. The more analysis that occurs in conjunction with the creation of field notes, the easier the project will be to complete (Lofland and Lofland 1984).

The fourth type of material in the field notes involves your *impressions and personal feelings*. Write down if you were scared, happy, rejected, or felt loved. Whom did you like and when did you feel completely stupid? One's feelings and impressions are often a source of analytic insights. Personal feelings have their roots in social events. If you are feeling certain things, others may be too, so this might be a worthy avenue to pursue. Also, your emotional reactions to people and events affect them and your interpretation of them. By having a record of your emotions you are in a better position to analyze the dynamics of interactions (Lofland and Lofland 1984).

The final elements in field notes are *things to think about and do*. Write down if you need to go back and collect a missing detail. If you have ideas that you want to follow up on, write these down (Lofland and Lofland 1984). What questions might be good to ask, and whom didn't you talk to today and would like to see tomorrow? You should review the "to do" list from the previous day before each observational period. Forward items not completed onto the next day's notes.

Given what you have already learned in this guide, can you guess when researchers start taking field notes? If your answer was that researchers begin taking field notes during the process of selecting the project, you are right! Field notes don't begin once you are in the field. Detailed descriptions of the decisions involved in selecting a particular project, setting, or group are written in the field notes. Preliminary goals and the reasons for them are written in the notes before you enter the field. The process of gaining entry is documented in the notes. As you arrive in the field, jot down in your field notes things that you are feeling. Here we see again how the step approach to field research is misleading: Field notes are not a step that you begin after completing several preliminary steps. Rather, field notes are created simultaneously with all the other processes of field research.

Some specific details of taking notes in the field might be helpful. A rule of thumb in the field is to do your interactions and observations in three-hour blocks. It is difficult to pay attention for much longer than that, and the amount we can retain at any one time is limited. Write your field notes as soon as possible after each observational period. The more time that elapses, the less you'll remember. If you interact with the members in the morning, write your field notes in the afternoon. It is usually OK to write your field notes the first thing in the morning if you've done your observations the evening before; fairly detailed memory can last during sleep as long as new experiences are kept to a minimum (Lofland and Lofland 1984). The worst situation for retention is when you attempt to create field notes for two observational periods at the same time. You will forget most of the events and the analytic insights you had during the first period, and you'll remember far less from the second than you should.

The number of pages of field notes generated per observational period varies greatly. Although there is no set number, the minimum seems to be around two single-spaced typed pages for each hour of observation. Although many of us think it is excessive, Lofland and Lofland (1984:67) suggest that approximately 13 pages of field notes should result from each hour's observation! It will take you at least as long to write your field notes as it took to observe, probably twice as long. Some find that three to four hours are spent writing field notes for every hour of field observations.

It is helpful to have access to a computer when creating each day's field notes. Word processing packages allow the flexibility of moving things about, and you are much more likely to go back and insert that stray thought with a computer than you are with a typewriter.

Regardless of what you use to type your field notes, keep them organized. Make sure they are dated and labeled. If you are using a computer, make a hard copy of those priceless field notes and back up your computer files in different locations.

If you think writing field notes sounds tedious, you are right. Most of it isn't particularly fun. Occasionally, you might enjoy writing about your emotional reactions to a given individual, but a lot of the creation of field notes is hard work. You will be tempted to put it off, but you have to persevere. Remind yourself that what is not written in the field notes that day will be lost forever. Once you form the habit of writing field notes, the task will seem easier (Lofland and Lofland 1984).

Leaving the Field

Field research, by definition, involves long-term interactions. While any project you do for class will probably last no more than a few days or weeks, most field research requires months or years. Many factors influence the decision to terminate the field portion of the research.

One's safety is a factor. Most agree that you should leave if your safety, either physical or psychological, is at risk. This is true whether you just arrived or have been there for months. You should also leave if the members in the setting no longer want you there.

Practical matters have a great deal of influence. Those of you who are doing field research for a class assignment will have a deadline imposed by the instructor. Some academics do fieldwork during summer months or during sabbaticals; we terminate the fieldwork portion when we are required to be back on campus. Running out of money is another reason field researchers leave the field.

Sometimes field researchers know it is time to stop the fieldwork when they feel that they are not learning anything new. One way you'll know when you are reaching this point is when the "things to do" portion of your field notes is getting smaller. More importantly, when you are drawing fewer and fewer analytic insights from active participation in the setting, it may be time for closure.

Whatever motivates the decision to leave, place the relationships that you have formed at the center of the process of exiting the setting. Think about what those in the setting need from you as well as what your needs are. By now, you probably have become close friends with several people. Some have come to depend upon you. A romantic relationship may even have formed.

One way of caring for these relationships is to discuss and plan your leaving with the members. Make sure that you have done all the things that you said you would before leaving. Discuss whether a party or some sort of ceremony would be enjoyed or whether you should just leave without fanfare. Some members may pull away from you in anticipation of your being gone. Respect their need for distance.

Another way of caring for these relationships is to plan your next contact with the members. Many of us continue to call, visit, or write the friends we've made during field research. At a minimum, many of us share a copy of the final report with the members in the setting. Give the members your best estimate of when they can expect to hear from you again and then make sure you follow up on what you promised.

Some of us believe that an important part of field research is having the members participate in the writing of and reacting to the final report. Therefore, you may need to schedule several additional meetings with the members. In our Midsouth County project, we occasionally have some of the women from Midsouth join us for work sessions at Virginia Tech, in addition to the frequent trips we make to Midsouth.

Exiting the setting used to have a fairly clear point of demarcation for the field researcher. As we give more primacy to our relationships in the field, we find that we don't so much terminate our field relationships as continue them in another form over greater distances.

CHAPTER HIGHLIGHTS

1. Formal and informal gatekeepers control access to a setting and the availability of data within the setting.

2. Gaining entry is negotiated and renegotiated throughout the research process.

3. Although sponsorship can facilitate research, it can also interfere with the research in complicated ways.

4. Arrival in a field setting is often filled with stress, fear, mistakes, and insecurities.

5. Key actors are individuals who act as guides or mentors to the field researcher.

6. Although informed consent is a goal of most field researchers, actually getting informed consent from everyone encountered in the field is problematic.

7. Trusting, reciprocal relationships are the basis of good field research.

8. Field researchers use all their senses during observations.

9. Field researchers observe the physical surroundings, the people, and the verbal and nonverbal behaviors that occur in a setting.

10. Field researchers use informal interviews to find out specific information of interest.

11. Informal interviews are reciprocal with both the researcher and the members engaging in dialogue.

12. Field researchers sometimes supplement data collection with techniques such as surveys, structured interviews, life histories, and focus groups.

13. Field notes are the backbone of collecting and analyzing field data.

14. Field notes consist of mental notes, jotted notes, fuller notes, and the full field notes themselves.

15. Field notes contain the chronological log of events, things previously forgotten, analytic ideas and inferences, impressions and personal feelings, and things to think about and do.

16. Field notes should be completed soon after each observational period, and they may take twice as long to write as the time to observe.

17. Regardless of what motivated the decision to terminate the fieldwork portion of the research, concern for the relationships formed in the setting should be primary while exiting.

EXERCISES

1. Pretend that you want to do research to understand the day-to-day interactions in a funeral home. Discuss the procedure that you would need to go through to gain the permission of the gatekeepers.

2. Someone from another methods class says to you that at least the issue of "gatekeepers" in field research is straightforward. She says, "All you have to do is get permission from the highest in authority, and then it's all taken care of." Respond in detail based upon what you've learned in this chapter.

3. Given all the discussion of ethics and reciprocal relationships in the field, do you think it is unethical for a researcher to engage in a romantic relationship with a member in the field? Defend your answer.

4. Go to a setting where you've never been before. Observe this setting for 10 minutes. Leave the setting and write as many things as you can remember. Then go to another setting where you've never been before. Observe this setting for 10 minutes. Take jotted notes about your observations while in the setting. Wait 24 hours and then write as many things as you can remember about this second setting without your notes. Then look at your notes and add any details you may have forgotten. What do you learn from this exercise?

5. Pick a topic and do a structured interview with a classmate. Then do an informal interview with another classmate on the same topic. Compare the procedures and your results.

6. Allan Roadburg writes that the form of interaction between the researcher and subjects is "unique insofar as neither party has any control over the fact that the termination of the relationship coincides with the termination of the research. If individuals wish to continue a relationship after the research has concluded, it will no longer be a researcher–subject relationship but will be based on different criteria" (1980:281). Do you agree with these statements? What are the implications of them for the field research process? Do you think the author of this guide would agree or disagree with Roadburg? Justify your answer.

7. Read the article in the appendix by Matthews Hamabata. Find an example from this article for as many items in the chapter highlights as you can.

4 And the Beat Goes On: The Art of Interpretation

This last chapter covered analysis, interpretation, understanding, and writing. However, these processes begin at the moment you first start to think about doing a field research project and continue during gaining entry, relationship building, interactions in the field, and writing the final report.

Making sense out of all your field experiences is difficult, and there are few rules to guide your analysis and writing and to help you gain analytic insights into the contours of everyday life in the setting. Consequently, if you were interested in field research because you believed it would be faster and easier to do than more quantitative forms of analysis, you are in for a surprise. Sometimes it is more fun, but I've never found it faster or easier.

Analysis

The following sections present some strategies that field researchers use to try to make analytic sense out of the massive amount of data they have experienced. These suggestions are not mutually exclusive or exhaustive; nor is there any guarantee that even if you use them all, you will have profound insights into the dynamics of the setting. Insights come not from strategies but from you. However, some of these strategies might help you think creatively and gain additional understanding about the group or setting you are studying.

Files

Lofland and Lofland (1984) advocate filing as an analytic aid, and I draw heavily from their expertise in the following paragraphs. **Filing** consists of separating your field notes, organizing them, and placing similar topics into folders. By filing your field notes into meaningful categories, you might start to see things, such as patterns and power relationships, that have previously gone unnoticed.

The practical aspects of filing are not difficult. I suggest that you file at least once a week and that you begin filing at the end of the week in which you select your project. How much time it will take you to file will vary. A great deal of time will be needed whenever you are deciding what folders you are going to create. Less time is needed for doing the actual filing. Having the right supplies can help you keep things organized. I like office supplies, so I have file folders, cardboard boxes, colored labels, highlighters, and scissors. I could achieve the same analysis with a pen, scissors, and lots of floor space to stack pages of notes, but it is more fun for me to work with these materials.

You will need multiple copies of your field notes. How many copies you will need depends upon such things as the number of people being observed and whether you decide to cut your notes into sections or use whole pages with the relevant passages circled. Since copying is expensive, start with the minimum suggested by Lofland and Lofland (1984) of two or three copies of each page of your field notes, but be prepared to make more. Most of you who will be doing field research for a class assignment should have little trouble getting access to a photocopying machine or a computer printer to make multiple copies. If you are doing your field research in a location where these technologies are not available, you need to have some other means for making multiple copies. Using carbon paper to produce multiple copies as you type each page of your field notes is low-tech, but it works. Make sure that you always set aside a master copy of your field notes, which you do not use for anything other than making copies.

Chronological Files

The first and easiest type of file you will keep is a **chronological file**. Each week make sure that you have a complete copy of your field notes filed in chronological order. If you are in the field for a long time, you may want to separate your chronological file into a series of folders by weeks, months, or years for easier access.

To facilitate your analysis, periodically skim or read these notes from beginning to end to help you see the big picture and notice changes over time. Also refer to your chronological file to help situate an event of interest in the appropriate larger context (Lofland and Lofland 1984:134–135). Thick descriptions, so essential to field research, are kept in the chronological file.

Analytical Files

Analytical files are the second type of file (Lofland and Lofland 1984). Each day's field notes contain an analytical section describing your ideas about such things as patterns, typologies, meanings, motivations, relationships among actors and events, and questions about theoretical possibilities. When you file, organize these analytical notes into meaningful groups.

The contents of analytical folders do not have to be mutually exclusive. That is, any one analytical insight might fit into several categories. When this occurs, simply make additional copies and file the same analytical note in several places, or at a minimum cross-reference it. Alternatively, an analytical note might start out in one analytical folder and then be moved to another as you gain insights into the setting.

Deciding on the themes for your analytical folders is the difficult part of creating an analytical file. I'll review some of the suggestions given by Lofland and Lofland (1984) on organizing your analytical folders. However, these are only suggestions to get you started, not procedures etched in stone. Periodically go through your analytical folders and see if you need to revise your filing systems by creating new analytical categories, subdividing files, or combining files.

One place to begin is to create an analytical folder that focuses on *meanings.* This folder contains your notes about (1) why you think people do what they do, (2) meanings members give to their actions, (3) how members define situations, (4) what worldviews, ideologies, and philosophies members hold, and (5) how members define, justify, and interpret their behavior (Lofland and Lofland 1984:73).

Another analytical folder might consist of insights about *roles.* There are lots of different types of roles, so you will need a folder for each type. For example, you could have folders consisting of your insights about role demands, role conflict, and multiple roles. Alternatively, you might have folders for formal roles such as being a point guard on a basketball team, being president of the Animation Club, and being a custodian.

Informal roles are often as important as formal roles, so you may want a folder for them. Think about some of the informal roles in your classes. Usually a few students take on the role of answering most of the questions. One student often takes on the role of the "shooter," the person who tries to antagonize the instructor. Others are "talkers." Some students take on the role of clarifying the test procedures and homework assignments. I'm sure you can think of other informal roles. If you were doing a field study of your classes, you might create a folder for each of these informal roles.

A third type of analytical file might include notes about *relationships*. You might create files about the types of relationships (such as friends, romantic, or business) seen in the setting. Alternatively, you could file your analytical insights into the stages of relationship formation—tentative beginnings, honeymoon, crisis, recovery, lasting contentment, and endings.

Many other types of analytical folders might be relevant to your setting. One set of analytical folders might contain insights about *groups*. For example, you might have folders that contain your notes on what cliques are formed in the group, the purposes of groups, the hierarchical structure among group members, and how the group hierarchy is maintained. Other folders might consist of your notes on *lifestyles*. For example, you might have folders on differences in the day-to-day lifestyles of your campus's theater/arts crowd, computer hackers, jocks, and sorority/fraternity members. Some field researchers keep insights about *rules, norms, and values* in analytical folders (Lofland and Lofland 1984:73). Your folders will depend upon you, your insights, and your settings. The above are only a few ideas to help you get started. The appropriate categories will emerge and be modified as you file.

Mundane Files

The Loflands call the third general type of file the **mundane file**. I tend to think of my mundane folders as my "people, places, events, and things" folders. What you call it, how you organize it, and what you put in it depends upon your research situation. Most likely, you will have a folder that contains the field notes for each key person; for notes about important events or activities; and a folder for notes on interactions and observations in different places. The goal is to file the notes about similar topics all in one place so that you can easily read all that you have collected about a particular person, place, or event without having to search the chronological record for every occurrence of this person, place, or event. Reading all you have written on a particular person, for example, may help you see things about this person that you did not notice when thinking about this person and others simultaneously.

I remember filing notes from informal interviews with women who had eating disorders. I had a folder for notes about families, but I quickly learned I needed to keep one folder for notes about fathers

and another for mothers. As these folders got bigger, I further classified each parent's folder into subtypes, such as absent fathers, mothers as best friends, and abusive fathers. The process of creating and
recreating folders helped me understand some differences in parental types that I had not noticed while doing the interviews.

Methodological Files

The fourth set of files is your **methodological file**. Your final report
will include explanations of your research procedures—how you
conducted your research, to whom you talked, ways in which you
protected confidentiality, and other procedural issues. Writing this
portion of the final report will be much easier if most of your notes
are already organized in the same file.

An essential part of analysis is the creation of the folders. The
process of thinking about what folders you need, what goes where,
and why it goes there is analysis. As you file, you will write additional notes about your justification for your filing system and the
insights that you are gaining. You will also read files from time to
time to concentrate on a particular aspect of your research. For example, studying your role files, you might understand something
that previously escaped you. You then create field notes about this
and include them in your files. Creating, filing, touching, reading,
shifting, sorting, and comparing your files are all thinking aids.

Typologies

Sometimes field researchers create typologies to help them discover
meaning in a social setting. A **typology** classifies similar events,
places, or people into discrete groups. For example, John Rosecrance
(1990) did a study of men who gamble on horses at race tracks. After
almost a year of observations, he found five types of regular horse
players:

1. Pros—the professional handicappers, reserved for the small per-
centage who have proved they can win consistently.

2. Serious players—those who have made a definite and demon-
strable commitment to earn their livelihood from wagering on
horses. They quit their regular jobs and begin playing the horses
as a full-time endeavor.

3. Bustouts—the individuals who exist in a continuing state of poverty. In racing argot they are "permanent residents of tap city."

4. Regulars—their employment situation allows them to attend the races during the week because they are either retired or flexibly employed.

5. Part-time players—includes players who are unable to attend regularly. Most of them have traditional weekly employment; they envision that after they retire they will become regulars. (1994:359–365)

Rosecrance's typology allowed him to see further important differences among the gamblers. For example, the regulars were more interested in maintaining track friendships than in making the big score. Anyone who posits a theory about why people gamble will need to address the diversity expressed in Rosecrance's typology.

Field researchers' creativity, luck, serendipity, experience, worldviews, research goals, and settings all affect their ability to create meaningful typologies. Typologies often emerge through the process of filing. However, since many researchers engage in this process independently of filing, I think it is important to describe typology formation as a distinct activity.

Let's imagine that you are doing field research on restaurants by observing multiple restaurants in your area. You might gain analytic insight by classifying the various restaurants into different types. What classification scheme you use will depend upon what you think is meaningful in the setting. For example, you might classify the restaurants by the type of food served—haute cuisine, fast food, health food, or ethnic food. In contrast, you might classify the restaurants by the type of patrons who frequent the establishments—business people, family groups, students, or wealthy diners. Alternatively, you might classify the restaurants by the way the food is served—take-out, buffet, drive-through, delivery, or table service. Another way to approach this imaginary research is to create a type based on the tasks that are done by the employees in the restaurants. You might have the categories cooks, servers, cleaners, and managers. These, of course, could be further subdivided.

Members in the setting often create their own types that help them make sense of their environment. When you interviewed the servers in the restaurant, did they use jargon that indicated customer styles—"in-and-outs," "lingerers," "flirters," and "complainers"? Member-created types are particularly useful for understanding the setting from their perspectives.

Researchers usually follow three guidelines when creating types. The classification scheme often is (1) mutually exclusive, (2) exhaustive, and (3) theoretically meaningful. Mutually exclusive categories classify everything into one and only one category. For example, a local restaurant serves fast health food. In the previous example of categories (haute cuisine, fast-food, health food, and ethnic food) this restaurant would fit into two categories. Therefore, these categories are not mutually exclusive. Sometimes this problem can be bypassed with a category of "mixed types." However, you probably need to rethink your classification criteria if a preponderance of cases end up in the mixed type category.

The categories should also be exhaustive: Every case needs to fit into one of the categories. For example, if you are doing field research on beach volleyball, you may originally select two categories based on the status of the players: amateur teams and professional teams. This might work fine until you observe a fund-raising tournament in which amateurs are paired with professionals. Because you have no place to put these teams, your scheme is not exhaustive. You need to add another category to account for these teams.

Third, the categories need to be theoretically meaningful. Although you could conceivably classify restaurants by the number of items hanging on the walls (restaurants with 10 or fewer wall decorations, 11 to 20, and 21 or more), I have a hard time imagining how such a classification scheme would tell us anything meaningful about the setting. If there is no social significance to the classification scheme, you need to find a new one.

Sometimes the overall scheme is fine, but a particular category in the typology is analytically problematic. For example, let's say that you decided to classify office personnel by whether they supervised others. Consequently, you might have two categories of workers—those who supervised others and those who didn't. This classification scheme might help you understand why some people see their jobs as more stressful but more prestigious than others. However, the category "supervising others" might not be as analytically meaningful as it could be. Supervising one temporary worker and supervising 40 permanent workers are probably not similar experiences. Therefore, the category "supervising others" is not theoretically meaningful. This category might be more useful to you if you broke it down into smaller gradations.

In practice, we find that using types often oversimplifies the dynamics in a setting. For example, a particular restaurant is not either a fast-food restaurant or a place that serves primarily students—it may be both. This combination of characteristics makes it different from another fast-food restaurant that serves primarily office workers. Therefore, a more reasonable way to classify restaurants is simultaneously on two or more types. When you classify on more than one dimension, you create a typology. What dimensions or types you use as the basis of your typology will depend upon what is theoretically meaningful to your study. Reread Rosecrance's typology of gamblers. Notice how it is based on more than one aspect of the gamblers.

Which typologies you use depends upon what you think is most analytically useful. Merely grouping people or places or events is not enough. You need to ask yourself a series of question. For this example, you might ask what characteristics restaurants in one group have in common that the restaurants in another group do not have. What can we learn about the restaurant trade, food, or people who eat out that we didn't realize before using a particular typology?

The goal of creating typologies is to gain additional understanding of day-to-day life in the setting. Putting activities, events, or individuals in boxes with snappy labels is insufficient to produce this understanding. Lofland and Lofland warn us:

> We must caution you . . . that typology construction can easily become a sterile exercise. Unless you perform it within the context of full and extensive knowledge of, and sensitivity to, the actual setting, it will reveal little or nothing. Arbitrary box building is not a substitute for a close feel for the actual circumstances. Typologizing is simply a tool to aid in systematic understanding. (1984:96)

Sometimes the inappropriate use of types and typologies can prevent understanding. This can happen when we attach labels to individuals that would not be appropriate if they exhibited the same characteristic in another setting. Elliot Liebow was careful to avoid this problem in his study of homeless women. He writes:

> In general, I have tried to avoid labeling any of the women as "mentally ill," "alcoholic," "drug addicted," or any other characterization that is commonly used to describe—or, worse, to explain—the homeless person. Judgments such as these are almost always made against a background of homelessness. If the same person were seen in another setting, the judgment might be altogether different. Like you, I know people who drink, people who do drugs, and bosses who have tantrums and treat their subordinates like dirt. They all have good jobs. Were they to become homeless, some of them would surely also become "alcoholics," "addicts," or "mentally ill." Similarly, if some

of the homeless women who are now so labeled were to be magically transported to a more usual and acceptable setting, some of them—not all, of course—would shed their labels and take their places with the rest of us somewhere on the spectrum of normality. (1994:xiii)

I want to reinforce a point made by Liebow in this quote. We need to be careful not to confuse a classification scheme with a causal factor. Betty Russell, in her study of homeless women, warns against using classifications that carry "simplistic notions of both causation and 'cures' for homelessness" (1991:30). Unfortunately, in her chapter "The Paths to Homelessness," she classifies the women in her study into three types: "mentally ill," "substance abusers," and "situationally homeless," implying that these are the characteristics that "predisposed" the women toward homelessness (1991:29). Her typology hides the impact of economic factors and abuse as predisposing factors for homelessness and imparts causal significance to factors that may be only correlates.

Another problem with types and typologies is that when used inappropriately they ignore the full range of characteristics exhibited by complex people. Again, I turn to Liebow to illustrate this point:

From the beginning, however, I paid little attention to mental illness, partly because I had difficulty recognizing it, and partly for other reasons. Sometimes mental illness seemed to be a "now-you-see-it, now-you-don't" phenomenon; some of the women were fine when their public assistance checks arrived, but became increasingly "symptomatic" as the month progressed and their money (security?) diminished, coming full circle when the next check arrived. . . . With a little patience on my part, almost all the women with mental or emotional problems were eventually and repeatedly accessible. Even on "bad" days, perhaps especially on "bad" days, these women sometimes said things that seemed to come, uncensored, from the depths of their emotional lives. (1994:xiii–xiv)

Reducing a particular woman to the category of mentally ill ignores how she constantly changes and ignores all the other dimensions of this woman. She also may be a mother, an artist, and a gifted conversationalist. These facets of her being get lost in the simple category of "mentally ill." Certainly, there are times when a typology based on psychiatric labels is useful, but we need to be careful because these labels have pitfalls.

Patterns

Another analytic aid is looking for patterns in the setting. What at first appears to be a mass of undifferentiated behaviors may, after careful observation, be seen as patterned. To discover patterns, look for events that occur regularly in a sequence. These patterns may take different shapes. Some may be like a circle—when the pattern is completed, the sequence begins again from the same starting point. Other events may occur sequentially—steps follow each other in a well-ordered fashion but do not return to a beginning point. Some events follow a spiral pattern, alternating between escalation and de-escalation, or crisis and resolution. If you can conceptually map these patterns or processes, you may gain insight into the setting.

Patterns are not easy to see because several different forms of patterned behavior may occur simultaneously within the same setting. Nonetheless, it is worthwhile to look for patterns. By observing and analyzing the patterns of everyday life, field researchers acquire a deeper understanding of and appreciation for how the "ornate human tapestry is woven together" (Fetterman 1989:93).

Diagrams

Sometimes diagrams, such as organizational charts, maps, or flowcharts, can give you analytical insight into a setting. You might make a flowchart of how people move through a system. You could draw an organizational chart of the power relationships embedded in the system. Maps of the social distances between groups in a setting are useful tools for generating analytical ideas. These diagrams would be drawn while you are observing in the setting, reinforcing the point that analysis strategies are used in the field as well as after the fieldwork is complete.

Metaphors

Metaphors are also useful analytic devices (Richardson 1994). Metaphors are comparisons, such as "the woman's skin was chocolate—smooth, rich, and silky." Trying to discover a metaphor that is appropriate to some aspect of your setting or group can help you see things in new ways. Start by asking yourself, what else is this like? What else does it remind me of? What kind of thing is it? Searching for a metaphor requires that you look at the setting or group from different conceptual angles to see if you have not recognized some of its dimensions. Look for new ways to view events in the setting that lead to new insight and understanding.

Some examples might help make this clearer. Viewing a juvenile court as an assembly line helps us to see how moving cases quickly through the court takes precedence over justice. As roads are built by a construction crew, the interpersonal dynamics may be more like a coffee klatch than a work group. Before thinking of the crew as a coffee klatch, you might have ignored the gossip and informal conversations among the group members. The metaphor allows you to see the important elements of social support, friendship networks, and interpersonal relationships among the crew. In our study with the women of Midsouth County, it would have been easy to see these women as victims of an oppressive system. While this is true, it is incomplete. These women are also like resisters in an occupied country. They share medicine, lie on forms, organize demonstrations, and hide relatives so as not to lose housing subsidies. Lacking the power to use formal channels, they use subterfuge to manipulate the system to get the help they need.

Miscellaneous Strategies

Numerous other analytic strategies are regularly employed by field researchers. To gain insight, we often review the literature. Danny Jorgensen (1989), for example, revisited the literature he had read earlier to help him understand emergent issues in his study of occultists. By reading literature you can learn what others have seen or felt about a setting similar to yours. This helps you think about how previous researchers' observations compare with what you are seeing and what might account for the similarities or differences. Do not feel constrained by what others have found; rather, use their insight as launching pads for your own (Jorgensen 1989).

Consulting with others is often valuable. You may want to talk to your instructor, best friend, partner, other researchers, or parents. Brainstorm, wax philosophical, extend scenarios to weird extremes, posit structural explanations, and make psychological diagnoses with someone who is a good conversationalist. Talking, like writing, can be a way of clarifying thoughts and gaining insights; but be extremely careful not to violate the confidentiality of anyone in the setting when you talk.

Some researchers are starting to use computers and special-purpose software to help them analyze their data. One of the best-known software packages is Ethnograph, produced by Qualis

Research Associates. There are several advantages to using computers as you analyze your data. For example, the software is able to quickly retrieve, display, and print text with similar themes. However, I suggest that you do not use computers or that you use them only as a supplement the first time you do field research, so that you will thoroughly understand the analysis process before relying on technological aid.

These are just a few of many strategies that can be used to help you gain insight. There is no substitute for hard work, thinking, reflection, writing, talking, and immersing yourself in the setting. It would be nice if there were manuals, like the ones you get for car repair or troubleshooting your computer, that you could use to gain analytic insight into your setting or group. Alas, such things do not exist, and that is what makes field research as much an art form as a method of social science research.

Regardless of which analytic strategy you employ, the goal is to understand meaning from the perspectives of the members. This understanding will obviously be mediated by who you are. You don't have to worry about finding some ultimate truth, and this should free you to be creative. I agree with Jorgensen that the best strategy for analytic insight is to "Use your imagination! The analysis of data leading to discovery requires creativity" (1989:110).

Extended Example of Using Multiple Analytic Strategies

Let's use a simple, contrived example to illustrate some of the suggestions just discussed. Pretend that I have required you to do field research for a week in the main sociology office at Typical University. Your fieldwork would take place in a fairly large space with probably no fewer than four people in the office at any one time and more coming and going in seemingly random fashion.

One of the first things you might do is to create a typology of the different types of people you see in the office. You might classify these people by their relationship to the university: permanent office staff, faculty members, undergraduates, and graduate students.

Much of your field research would consist of discovering the multiple roles and overlapping patterns of activities in this setting. One set of roles and related patterned behavior would be that of the permanent office staff. You'd learn that Leigh handles undergraduate concerns; Jane is responsible for graduate student records. Elaine is the administrative assistant who handles the finances, schedules, and requests of the department head. Drawings of the organizational structure of the office might give you a clearer sense of the hierarchical relationships among the staff.

More importantly, you would want to get at the underlying meanings that are embedded in the office staff's perceptions of their jobs. You might search for meaning by looking for the patterns in work responsibilities. Do they do the same tasks every day in the same order? This would help you determine if their jobs are routine, possibly lacking in challenge and opportunities to be creative. Are some times of day, weeks, or months busier than others? This could help you locate sources of stress and tension that might lead to conflict or cohesion. In what order is work done and who decides what the work patterns will be? Flowcharts of work requests might help you learn how much autonomy they have, which could affect job satisfaction. You would compare your answers to these questions with what they told you about their jobs during informal interviews. Consequently, you would look in the appropriate files to help you gain insight.

As you reviewed your notes on who does what when, you might see exceptions to the patterns you had previously seen. Your next analytic task would be to see if these exceptions followed a pattern. It might be the case, for example, that Leigh randomly decides to help Jane. However, after studying all your field notes from your mundane files on when Leigh helped Jane, you might see that Leigh's behavior is not random. Leigh might expand her duties during busy times, during lunch hours, or with some faculty members. She might be more helpful when she is trying to avoid an unpleasant task of her own. Consequently, even the exceptions might be patterned, and fairly predictable, giving you insight into the setting.

What would it mean, for example, if you found that Leigh helps Jane more than Jane helps Leigh? It could mean lots of things:

1. Leigh is underutilized.
2. Leigh is more efficient.
3. Leigh's work is more flexible.
4. Jane's work is more important.
5. Leigh is trying to learn Jane's job.
6. Leigh likes to have her hands in whatever is going on.
7. Leigh is a really nice person who likes to help whenever she can.

Some of these reasons might indicate that the office is a pleasant place to work; others might indicate that conflict is brewing. The goal of analysis is not just to describe when Leigh helps. Rather, it is to get at the social meaning, as perceived by all concerned, of her helping. You need to analyze Leigh's behavior within the context in which it occurs. Certainly, you would want to look in your analytical files to see what you've written. By reading your field notes, reviewing your interviews, by reorganizing your files, and by discovering patterns, you might gain some insights about what it is like to work in this office setting.

Sometimes you will think that you understand a particular pattern, but further observation will indicate that the pattern is more complex than you previously thought. For example, you may see that faculty are autonomous in the office. Faculty come and go for a variety of reasons, but they do not disturb the office staff. They get office supplies, print something, make a photocopy, and get coffee filters for the machine in the faculty lounge. Because you perceive that faculty and staff operate independently of each other, you may conclude that status differences are not an issue in this office. With further observation, however, you may find that between self-sufficient movements, faculty have many requests. They may ask Leigh to pull a file on an undergraduate student; they may need a fax sent; they may need an exam typed; they may need to be reimbursed for travel expenses; and they may need to make an appointment to see the department head. You start to think of this setting in terms of the metaphor that the office staff are emergency medical personnel who respond to faculty crises. Consequently, you revise your earlier conclusion that faculty do not change the routine office patterns to a new interpretation that faculty are allowed to change staff patterns for certain requests. Status differences then reappear for consideration in the rest of your analysis.

Next, you might create a typology of requests in order to help you understand the impact on the office personnel of each type of request. For example, typing exams may be considered an undesirable task by the staff, so the staff might employ avoidance strategies when they think a faculty member might ask them to type one. In contrast, requests for travel expenses reimbursement might be handled in good spirits because of the chance to socialize by sharing travel stories.

Further analysis might reveal yet another office dynamic. Through reading the professors' folders in your mundane file, you find that two faculty members will not get their own office supplies, will not make their own photocopies, ask to have coffee made, and interrupt the office staff at any time for anything. You then need to understand the social meaning behind these events. Are these faculty new and don't know how to do these things? Are these faculty members high-ranking members of the department who see these sorts of tasks as beneath their dignity? Are these faculty members highly sociable and so make requests of the staff as an excuse to chat with them? Have the staff insisted upon meeting these two faculty members' every request because the two are well liked? To get the answers to these questions you might go to the chronological log. What have you written about the body language of the staff when these faculty members are in the office? What is the tone and text of conversations when the requests are made? What happened after the faculty left the office? How do these observations match what the office staff have said about these faculty during informal interviews? Again, your goal is to get at social meaning, not just description.

You might use maps of traffic patterns to help you understand the social meaning in this setting. Your map might indicate that most office traffic goes to Leigh's desk and stops. Only a few people other than the staff move about the room. By making maps for each role, you would discover that the undergraduates rarely move freely about the office. However, on some of your diagrams you might find this rule doesn't apply to all undergraduates. For example, you might notice that one undergraduate goes farther into the office than other undergraduates. By asking about this exception, you discover that this privilege has been granted to the Sociology Club President. Maps of the graduate students traffic patterns might show you that they have more freedom to move in the office than undergraduates, but they do not wander over to the supply cabinet, nor are they ever spotted near the copy machine. This might indicate that the department has a limited budget and reserves these valuable resources for faculty only. Analysis of traffic patterns leads to greater understanding of status differences and the importance of office security.

From reading this example you should have a clearer idea of how to employ some of the analytic strategies described in this chapter. You should also see that analysis occurs while you are immersed in the setting.

Writing

Writing is an essential part of all phases of field research (Denzin and Lincoln 1994:479). You do not write up your results after your analysis is done; the act of writing *is* analysis of the setting or social group. I like Laurel Richardson's view on writing and field research:

> Although we usually think about writing as a mode of "telling" about the social world, writing is not just a mopping-up activity at the end of a research project. Writing is also a way of "knowing"—a method of discovery and analysis. . . . I write because I want to find something out, I write in order to learn something that I didn't know before I wrote it. I was taught, however, as perhaps you were, too, not to write until I knew what I wanted to say, until my points were organized and outlined. (1994:516, 517)

Similar to Richardson, I view writing as yet another analytic strategy used by field researchers to gain insight into a setting. If you are not constantly writing about your field research, you are not doing field research. Writing, doing, and understanding are all basically the same thing in field research.

Good Writing

The fact that writing is an analytic strategy in field research does not relieve you from outlines, grammar rules, thesis sentences, or any of the other conventions of good writing. You probably know the rules of good writing—for example, avoid passive verbs, eliminate unnecessary words, make sure the subject and verb agree, and avoid run-on sentences. Even if these rules sound familiar, I suggest that you purchase a style guide to refresh your memory and to have available when you aren't sure of something.

Because using metaphors is an analytic aid, read the sections about them in your writing guides. When you write, avoid clichéd metaphors. For example, business leaders talk about the need to be team players who avoid end runs; these are metaphors borrowed from sports. Military metaphors are common; medical personnel talk about using weapons to fight disease. Academics sometimes use construction metaphors to talk about the structure, framework, and foundation of an argument. Again, I agree with Richardson:

> Using old, worn-out metaphors, although easy and comfortable, after a while invites stodginess and stiffness. The stiffer you get, the less flexible you are. You invite being ignored . . . and you will bore people. (1994:524)

Notice how a change in the following metaphors changes the tone of the writing. Someone that provides assistance can be an aide-de-camp or a midwife. Many options can be an arsenal or a spice rack of choices. Thinking of new metaphors enhances your analytic processes; it can also make your writing more interesting. I think making one's writing interesting is a legitimate goal for a field researcher:

> The writer's object is—or should be—to hold the reader's attention. . . . I want the reader to turn the page and keep on turning to the end. (Tuchman 1989)

After all, what's the purpose of doing research if the final report is so tedious that no one bothers to read it? Although academicians are often criticized for inaccessible writing, many scholars know this doesn't have to be true and are changing their writing accordingly. In fact, a new journal called *Writing Sociology* focuses on making writing more appealing for readers.

I like what my colleague Lou Middleman has to say about good writing:

> Two classes of adjectives describe "good" writing. The first consists of words like *clear* and *coherent*. . . . Writing is *clear* when it transmits meaning as a clean, optically flat window transmits light, without distortion or interference. And writing is *coherent* when its parts join to form something that is obviously *one thing* and not just anything at all. (1987:2)

Another important point made by Middleman is that what constitutes good writing also depends upon the audience. He writes:

> Good writing is writing that suits the writer's purpose and the reader's expectations; it suits a sender's purpose and a receiver's ability and willingness to receive. That is, good writing is "good" relative to a particular intention and a particular rhetorical situation. (1987:2)

One way to achieve good writing is by writing and then rewriting many times. Most of us rewrite every paragraph and sometimes every line several times before we consider something finished. We reorganize sentences and paragraphs numerous times. We change individual words in a sentence. Then we go back and edit and rewrite again.

Rewriting does not just improve the writing: It improves our thoughts. Through the process of rewriting we realize what we are trying to say. I would be surprised if your first draft, or even second or third draft, is an acceptable final project. Even if you are a good writer in the sense of not making grammatical errors, multiple drafts are still usually required to clarify thinking. You may find that you enjoy writing more if you start to think of it as a way to understand, not simply as a way to communicate what you understand.

The more you write, the better you will be at it, and the more you will benefit from it. I suggest that you write every day to find out if Ueland's views are true:

> Writing, the creative effort, should come first—at least for some part of every day of your life. It is a wonderful blessing if you will use it. You will become happier, more enlightened, alive, impassioned, light-hearted, and generous to everybody else. Even your health will improve. Colds will disappear and all the other ailments of discouragement and boredom. (1938)

Although Ueland's claims may be slightly exaggerated, I hope that you can learn how to have fun with and enjoy writing.

Final Report Writing Styles

Academic writing usually follows a style or pattern consistent with the expectations of the discipline. For example, look through several issues of the *American Sociological Review*. While you will see a great deal of variation in topics, you will note that the style and presentation are similar from article to article. Most of the articles using a quantitative method have similar headings: an abstract, a statement of the problem or introduction, probably a theory section and certainly a review of the literature, and sections labeled hypotheses, methods, results, and conclusions.

This formulaic approach is less rigid for research that is classified primarily as qualitative. Nonetheless, the traditional approach to writing the final report of a field research project, sometimes called **realist tales** (Van Maanen 1988), contains some common conventions. First, the members in the setting are written about, but any details about the author are absent from the body of the text. The text is written as if anyone who was there would have experienced the same thing, so characteristics of the author, even his or her presence, are irrelevant to the tale. Second, realist tales contain concrete details of what is done, how often, in what order, and by whom. The goal is not to document everything that occurred but rather to identify the typical activities and patterns of behavior in the setting. Third, realist tales present the members' points of view. The author includes quotations, interpretations by members, summaries of informal interviews, and members' accounts and interpretations of events. Finally, realist tales include interpretations of the setting. The field research is written as if the meaning of the setting is now understood from the perspectives of the members in the setting.

In contrast to realist tales, Laurel Richardson argues that as the methodology of field research has changed, so have the writing practices of field researchers. She describes many current final reports of field research as **experimental writing**, not realist tales. Experimental writing comes in lots of shapes and sizes. What it all has in common, she believes, is the violation of prescribed realist tale conventions (1994:520).

Experimental writing begins with the premise that what one comes to know is not independent of the knower. What we write is only a part of what we have learned in a particular situation and is not independent of ourselves as researchers. Further, our influence or presence is also only partial, since we never reveal all of ourselves in our writing either. These beliefs allow us to free ourselves from a goal of "getting it right" to what Laurel Richardson calls "getting it differently contoured and nuanced" (1994:521).

Experimental writing among field researchers includes many different forms. One form is the *narrative of the self.* A narrative of the self does not read like a traditional ethnography because it uses the writing conventions of fiction. Narratives of the self are specific stories about particular events. The field researcher is freed to "exaggerate, swagger, entertain, make a point without tedious documentation, relive the experiences, and say what might be unsayable in other circumstances" (Richardson 1994:521).

Ethnographic fictional representations are a second type of experimental writing by field researchers. Those who write narratives of the self use the techniques of fiction writers; the writers of this second type go one step further by writing fiction. They tell a story about the self, group, and culture being studied. They create a series of characters, and cultural norms are conveyed through the characters in the story (Richardson 1994:521–522).

A third type of experimental writing is the *poetic representation.* Those who use this form argue that when people talk, their speech is closer to poetry than it is to sociological prose. Therefore, writing interviews "as poems honors the speaker's pauses, repetitions, alliterations, narrative strategies, rhythms, and so on." Richardson suggests that

> . . . poetry may actually better represent the speaker than the
> practice of quoting snippets in prose. Setting words together in

new configurations lets us hear, see, and feel the world in new dimensions. Poetry is thus a practical and powerful method for analyzing the social world. (1994:522)

Ethnographic drama is a fourth type of experimental writing used by some field researchers. Richardson writes:

When the material to be displayed is intractable, unruly, multisited, and emotionally laden, drama is more likely to re-capture the experience than is standard writing. (1994:522)

When using this form, the end product of the field research might be performed instead of written.

Finally, another category of experimental writing is classified as **mixed genres**. Field researchers draw upon "literary, artistic, and scientific" writing styles. An example of this is Margery Wolf's *A Thrice-Told Tale* (1992). She retells the same events as a fictional story, as field notes, and as a social scientific paper. Others have written final field research reports as combinations of journal entries, poems, essays, photographs, drawings, and annotated transcripts.

Experimental forms of writing are not for everyone. They are published in mainstream qualitative journals such as the *Journal of Contemporary Ethnography* and *Qualitative Sociology* and by major presses such as Routledge, University of Chicago Press, and Sage Publications. However, they are still not the standard style. Many field researchers situate their writing between realist tales and experimental writing.

Most field researchers write more reflectively and more self-consciously than before. It is rare not to have a sense of the author. We analyze, reflect, discuss, ponder, and wax philosophical about who we are and how that affected what we experienced in a setting. We have moved from writing about the other to letting others speak for themselves. However, letting others speak for themselves is still affected by the particular dynamics of our being in the setting. Further, the notion of other has eroded as more collaborative models of research have developed. Many of us no longer think in terms of ourselves as authors and the members as the other, but rather in terms of all of us working together.

Experiment to find your own style of writing. I agree with Laurel Richardson that "nurturing our own voices releases the censorious hold of 'science writing' on our consciousness, as well as the arrogance it fosters in our psyche" (1994:518). As we write, we need to remember that what we write is affected by who we are, our biography, our status characteristics, and our personalities. What we write is situationally specific and affected by the relationships we formed in the field. It is easy to forget these things when we attempt to write like a scientist who has found the truth.

Try writing in several different styles to find the one that suits you. For example, when I began writing this guide, I needed to select my style. I could have written in the language of social scientists. This might have been a typical sentence: "According to Kincheloe and McLaren (1994), postmodern ethnographers eschew claims to universality, positing instead that truth claims are discursively situated and implicated in relation to power." Alternatively, I could have written this guide as a poem, play, or television show with characters explaining how to do field research.

Instead of these formats, I chose a conversational style. I wanted you, the reader, and myself as author to engage in an imaginary dialogue about field research. I have spoken to you directly many times in this text, asking you questions and anticipating your questions. I have shared stories and my impressions of things. Sometimes I used the formal language of social science because it is useful for you to know the specialized vocabulary of field researchers. However, I have tried to present this vocabulary in a way that is easy to understand. As you write, you need to find your style, taking into account who your audience will be.

Content and Structure of the Final Report

What you include in your final report depends upon your goals, the setting, your biography, and a host of other factors. The following generic suggestions will probably be negotiated with your class instructors, thesis committee, journal editor, sponsor, or book publisher. Consequently, remember that I am providing you with a menu of suggestions to choose from—not a rule book to follow.

Introduction

It helps the reader if you begin with an introduction that gives an overview of where you are going. However, since you won't know where you are going until you discover that through your writing, the introduction will be one of the last things you write for your final report. You won't know what to include in the introduction until at least most of the report is finished.

History

Early in your report you might discuss the history of the setting or group. Some of this information will come from written sources—newspaper stories, statistical abstracts, and brochures. I usually glean a fair amount of history from reading journal articles or books. You will also collect information about the history and context from informal interviews with members in the setting.

Narrative

Part of your final report can be a narrative of what happened. Often this is presented in chronological order. The meanings and interpretations of events can be embedded within the narrative. An alternative to chronological order is to organize your narrative around key events, roles, patterns, relationships, or typologies.

Supporting Documentation

Your final report should include data that support your analyses. These data might consist of verbatim quotations, maps, or lengthy selections from your field notes. Some who read your work may still disagree with your interpretation of the data, but it should be clear what evidence you used to make your conclusions. For example, Mindy Stombler and Patricia Yancey Martin (1994) did a field research project on fraternity little sister organizations. They conclude that fraternity little sister organizations provide a formal structure on campus in which female disadvantage is institutionalized through organizations that encourage women's subordination, exploitation, and dependence. They weave some verbatim quotations throughout their final report to support their conclusions:

> "Personality maybe, it's minuscule. What is important is your body and your whole outlook on the guys. Once we paid our monetary dues we didn't have to do anything except look good." (1994:157)

> "Like we had to bring things, that's another thing that really bothered me about NM. Like we had to bring things to rush like cokes, chips, stuff like that. We had to bring cokes and stuff every day of [men's] rush. It got expensive . . . if we didn't do stuff for our little brothers they got on our case. It was more like to NM we were there to serve." (1994:164)

> "But it was not that; plenty of us had no little brothers. I had two but lots of girls didn't have any. . . . It was because she

wasn't good-looking. She was the best little sister in the group. . . . [T]his was my good friend and she was an awesome little sister, fun to be with, at every party, she never got drunk or out of control or anything like that. There was just no reason for it. It really upset me [when she was permanently expelled]." (1994:158)

Stombler and Martin also included the voices of women who felt they benefited from the organizations:

"We had guys coming up to us all the time. They really wanted us there. We couldn't believe this. My first week up at school, I had a couple of people from the fraternity asking me out and that would happen like in a year's time back at home. I was pretty flattered. We were treated like queens." (1994:159)

"You really felt like you were part of something when you went there, right from the start." (1994:160)

"They treat you like a family . . . like I am his [true] little sister. God forbid anybody had said anything to me or badmouthed me. It was like, 'I'll kill you.' " (1994:162)

Part of their analysis was trying to understand the divergent voices. For example, they discussed the benefits to individual women (a sense of belonging) versus costs to women as a group. Their analysis was strengthened, not weakened, by including data that ran counter to their conclusions. Their readers were given the chance to weigh their arguments and analysis with data from the setting.

Also, field researchers accept that people have different interpretations of reality. A final report that implied that everyone was seeing the same things in the same way would be suspect. Field research allows for the exploration of difference rather than masking it as sometimes happens in statistical analysis. Statistical analysis reduces respondents to an average or mean with a standard deviation often given as the only indicator of difference. Field researchers highlight differences and use them to get at the complexity of social life. However, it is inappropriate to take an atypical statement and try to pass it off as representing most individuals in the setting.

Part of the supporting documentation is placing the analysis in context. You may have heard real estate agents say "location, location, location," implying that the value of a house is determined more by its location than the quality of the house. The equivalent for the field researcher is the context in which something was said or occurred. For example, a comment made among close friends has a different meaning and social impact than the same comment made to a person in authority. Consequently, it isn't enough to give a verbatim quotation without explaining the context in which the statement was made. When doing your analysis and writing the final report, you will go again and again to your field notes and chronological file to try to understand the dynamics within the context in which they occurred.

Retaining the Speaker's Voice

The voices of the members in the setting should be used in the final report to allow readers to make their own judgments about what was meant. Using the members' voices (word choices, language, and style) also gives insight into who they are. For example, two characters created by P. G. Wodehouse (1976) and his modified dialogue show how two people can express essentially the same thought while saying something radically different about themselves. The first speaker is Bertram Wooster, a young man of privilege, and the second speaker is his butler, Jeeves.

> *Bertram:* Gosh, I'm feeling good today. Mind you, don't know how long it will last. It's often when one's feelin' good that the storm clouds begin doing their stuff.

> *Jeeves:* Very true, sir. Full many a glorious morning have I seen flatter the mountain tops with sovereign eye, kissing with golden face the meadows green, gilding pale streams with heavenly alchemy, Anon permit the basest clouds to ride with ugly rack on his celestial face and from the forlon world his visage hide, stealing unseen to west with this disgrace.

> *Bertram:* Exactly. I couldn't have said it better myself. You've got to watch out for a change in the weather. Still, you've got to be happy while you can.

> *Jeeves:* Precisely, sir. Carpe diem, the Roman poet Horace advised. The English poet Herrick expressed the same sentiment when he suggested that we should gather rosebuds while we may. Your elbow is in the butter, sir.

> *Bertram:* Oh, thank you, Jeeves.

If I had been present during this conversation, I could have summed it up by saying that Jeeves and Bertram talked about how one needs to be prepared for quick and unexpected changes in the weather. While I would be technically correct, my summary would have lost most of what was going on in this exchange. Could you guess from my summary which of the speakers is more casual in his approach to life and which is more formal? Probably not. Could you guess from my summary which one of the characters is most likely to have his elbow in the butter? Probably not. However, the original voices of the characters make it not at all surprising that Bertram, who speaks in casual tones, has the encounter with the butter, and not Jeeves, who is much more formal in his speech.

Once people have spoken, the job of the field researcher is to provide analysis and interpretation that go beyond a mere recounting. We record the voices and insight of the people within the setting and then step back, providing the context and the holistic approach that allow for these voices to be interpreted in broader ways.

Locating Yourself

You may have noticed an inherent conflict in field research. A goal of field research is to understand a setting from the perspectives of the members. However, this goal conflicts with the assumptions held by most field researchers that we have no privileged place to claim authoritative knowledge, that our truths are only partial truths, and that we can at best represent, but never truly know, the perspectives of the members. Although we cannot resolve this conflict, many field researchers deal with it by including in their final reports their reflections on the conflict. This is how Elliot Liebow addresses this issue in his study of homeless women.

> This perspective—indeed, participant observation itself—raises the age-old problem of whether anyone can understand another or put oneself in another's place. Many thoughtful people believe that a sane person cannot know what it is to be crazy, that a white man cannot understand a black man, a Jew cannot see through the eyes of a Christian, a man through the eyes of a woman, and so forth in both directions. In an important sense, of course, and to a degree, this is certainly true; in another sense, and to a degree, it is surely false, because the logical extension of such a view is that no one can know another, that only John Jones can know John Jones, in which case social life would be impossible.
>
> I do not mean that a man with a home and family can see and feel the world as homeless women see and feel it. I do mean, however, that it is reasonable and useful to try to do so.

Trying to put oneself in the place of the other lies at the heart of the social contract and of social life itself. (1994:xiv, xv)

When writing a report, field researchers try to explain how what they have learned in the field reflects their images, understandings, and interpretations of the setting (Denzin and Lincoln 1994). More simply, what we come to know in a setting is affected by who we are, including our status characteristics, our personality, our appearance, and our expertise. Consequently, for your readers to understand your writing in the final report, you need to locate yourself in the final report.

Kristine Baber and Katherine Allen, two highly respected family scholars, do a good job of locating themselves in their research:

In this book, we write about women in both concrete and analytic ways. Our perspective is both informed and limited by our own unique life experiences. . . . We have been trained and socialized in a privileged society of scholars, but we are critical of the ways in which our experiences and knowledge as women have been devalued and distorted. . . . Our perspectives, choice of topics, and choice of examples are limited by our own personal and intellectual heritages. We are both white, middle-class, educated, feminist women who were trained in the early 1980s in family studies programs, and we teach in similar academic departments at state universities. Our differences in perspective about women and families come from our personal histories and marital and parental careers. . . . One of us (Baber) is in a long-term marriage and is child free; the other (Allen) has been married and divorced and is now coparenting a young child in a committed relationship with another woman. . . . We have worked closely to understand just what we mean by women's solidarity in the context of their diversity so that we do not treat diversity as just a mark on a demographic checklist. (1992:viii)

Locating yourself also means that you do not have to hide ambivalent feelings in your final report. You can say that you are unsure of an analytical insight if that is the case. You can tell your readers how you were so miserable the whole time you were in the field that you didn't always observe the way you had intended to. You can say that you were offended by what you were observing or were surprised and ashamed for never having seen things before that you saw for the first time in the setting. In fact, not only can you include these sorts of things in your final report, you should include them.

There is a difference, however, between presenting one's social and emotional involvement in the setting as data and writing narcissistic and self-indulgent accounts of one's every mood in the setting. Punch warns against opening "the floodgates for sentimental, emotional, pseudo-honest accounts detailing every nervous tremor and moment of depression or elation" (1986:14).

Methodological Details

The final report usually contains details of the procedures used during the research. Readers need to know such things as how long you were in the field, whether you used a tape recorder, and how you handled informed consent. Sometimes these details are embedded within the text of the final report; they can also be included in a methodological appendix. When you write this section of your final report, you will be pleased with yourself if you created a methodological file during your research.

Sharing Your Results with the Members

A successful analysis rings true with both the members in the setting and colleagues who are experts in the area (Fetterman 1989:21). There is a difference, however, between a description that rings false, which probably means something is seriously wrong, and a controversial interpretation of the setting, which is to be expected (Fetterman 1989:21–22). Many field researchers allow members in the setting to react to and comment on the analysis. Some field researchers include the members' reactions in the final report.

In his study of homeless women, Liebow (1994) had two homeless women and the director of a shelter write comments on his manuscript. He edited their comments for length but changed none of their language. He used some of the comments that confirmed his viewpoints and all of the comments that disagreed with what he had written, that disagreed with each other, or that offered a different perspective. He included their comments on the relevant pages in italics.

Judith Stacey shared her manuscript with two members of the families she studied. She writes:

> In the interval since we had spoken last, Pam and Dotty both had been reading drafts of the chapters I had written about their respective families. Neither was entirely pleased with what she

had read. Dotty wished that I had not portrayed her family's plight in such disheartening terms. It was a depressing story, she agreed, but she would have given it a "more Pollyannaish" cast. However, Dotty observed, "It's your book, not mine." Pam had a comparable response. She had not yet finished reading all of the chapters, in part because she was finding doing so such an uncomfortable experience. Pam had detected a number of minor factual errors in my portrait of her family. . . . Like Dotty, however, Pam had concluded that my textual errors were not her business. "After all," she reminded me, the book "is really not my baby; it's yours." (1991:xiii–xiv)

By providing these comments, Stacey tells us several important things. First, the members did not totally agree with what she had written. This is OK; it is rare to find otherwise. Second, neither Dotty nor Pam claimed ownership of the final project. This tells us that the women may have felt that they were written "about" or "for," but they did not feel like collaborators in this project. Third, we know that Stacey stayed in contact with these women after she left the field. Fourth, because Stacey shared these comments with her readers, she seems to be an honest researcher. Finally, her final report made Pam uncomfortable, reminding us of the seriousness of ethical issues in the way we write and share our final report.

Ethical Issues in the Final Report

Many ethical issues appear in conjunction with the final report. Because many of them have been previously discussed in this guide, I will reinforce only two of them here. First, field researchers need to be sure that no harm comes to the members, the setting, themselves, their relationships with the members, and their professions. One way this is done is by taking extreme care to protect members' confidentiality in the final report. For example, using names and locations in the final report is a clear violation of confidentiality. A more common breach of confidentiality is using pseudonyms or vague references that are insufficient to disguise the source or place. For example, the location of a research setting can sometimes be determined once the institutional affiliation of the researcher is known because researchers tend to choose sites close to home. This has led to the identification of "Middletown" as Muncie, Indiana, "Rainfall West" as Seattle, and "Westville" as Oakland, California (Punch 1994). Further, what reads like an interesting but harmless detail, such as the paint scheme on a motorcycle or the type of microbiological research being done, may be sufficient for members who are thousands of miles from the research setting to be able to identify a person. Liebow explains in his preface how he protected the confidentiality of the homeless women he studied:

> Although the names of the women, the shelters (except those in D.C.), and many place names were changed for obvious reasons, most of the women will be known to one another and perhaps to others as well. Where a faithful physical description would be likely to identify a woman to family or friends or others, as in Elsie's case (only one external ear, no ear canals, a weight of over 300 pounds), I sought specific permission to use it. In two cases I substituted one disabling characteristic for another. (1994:xviii)

Second, field researchers need to be honest in the final report. Those who read the final report rarely have access to field notes or transcripts of interviews. The reader knows what quotations were included in the final report but has no way of knowing what was excluded if the field researcher doesn't tell us (Punch 1986). Consequently, the reader has no choice but to trust the field researchers to give an honest account of the research. It is unethical to misrepresent such things as one's data, one's relationship with members in the field, and how the research was done.

Conclusions and Appendixes

The final report often ends with a conclusion and appendixes. The conclusion is sometimes written like the introduction, but instead of saying where you are going you say where you have been. You might repeat major themes and issues in the conclusion. Policy implications or other broad implications of your research might be discussed. I like to think of the conclusions as my chance to get on a soapbox and get passionate about my topic. What type of conclusion is appropriate depends upon why the field research was done.

Appendixes can contain anything that you think is important and interesting but that didn't fit smoothly in the main text. Liebow, for example, has five appendixes in his book (1994): "Where Are They Now?" "Life Histories," "How Many Homeless?" "Social Service Programs," and "Research Methods and Writing." Betty Russell has seven appendixes in her book on homeless women (1991), many of which contain details on the survey to supplement her field research. Sometimes methodological details are collected in an appendix rather than being in the main text. Don't forget that ethical issues also apply to appendixes. If you include field notes or interview transcriptions in your appendixes, make sure that you do so in a way that protects confidentiality.

Final reports vary in length. Some field research is published as books; other authors write journal articles of approximately 25 pages. In our study of Midsouth County, we are producing an information packet, journal articles, and a formal report to the Women's Research Institute, which helped fund this project. If you are doing a field research project for a class, the length of the final report will probably be negotiated with your instructor.

Summary

We have traveled together a long way on our journey into field research. You should now have a better sense of how to gain an understanding of everyday life in a setting through long-term interactions with the setting's members. I hope this guide both has given you an appreciation for the complexity and utility of field research and will serve as a handrail to steady your steps into the exciting but difficult terrain of your own field research project.

I want to reassure you that in spite of the difficulties and ambiguities of this type of research, you are capable of doing a field research project. Field research is not an activity that should be restricted to an elite few. I strongly encourage you to try a field research project because doing field research is the best way to learn how to do field research.

CHAPTER HIGHLIGHTS

1. Analysis, or the art of interpretation, is not distinct from the other processes of doing field research.
2. Organizing one's field notes into files is a useful analytic aid.
3. Field researchers often create chronological files, analytic files, mundane files, and methodological files.
4. Field researchers sometimes use typology construction as an analytic aid.
5. When used incorrectly, typologies can misrepresent the complexity of social life.

6. Searching for multiple patterns of behaviors and events in a setting is a useful way of attempting to gain insight into the setting.

7. Diagrams, such as maps, flowcharts, and organizational charts, are useful analytic tools for the field researcher.

8. Field researchers use writing as a way of understanding, not just a way of reporting what they understand.

9. Good writing requires a lot of rewriting.

10. Field researchers need to find the writing style for the final report that works best for them and their audience.

11. The supporting documentation for conclusions, such as verbatim quotations or sections from the field notes, needs to be included in the final report.

12. The final report should contain reflections about who you are as a researcher and how that affected what you came to know about a setting.

13. Field researchers frequently share their final report with members to see if it rings true to them.

14. Ethical issues are salient throughout the field research process.

EXERCISES

1. Pick a public setting. Observe for one hour and map the traffic patterns of people in the setting. Discuss what you learned and what you needed to know to make your maps more useful.

2. Collect the front page of a local newspaper for five days in a row. Using scissors, floor space, and anything else you need, organize all the articles into meaningful groups. What did you learn about the priorities in the news and about creating files and typologies? Compare your analysis with those of your classmates.

3. Using the journals in your library that publish field research, find an example of a traditional style of field research report and an example of experimental writing. Discuss the differences, the implications of these styles for understanding, and the impact that they had on you as a reader.

4. Pretend that you are writing this guide. Write at least two pages of text in your own style.

5. Write a two-page letter to a friend or family member. Using a writing guide, grade your letter. Find all the grammatical errors,

misspellings, wordiness, and so on that you can. Then rewrite it. Trade your letter with a member in the class and grade each others' letters.

6. Select five published accounts of field research from the same journal. Copy the section headings used in these articles. Then select another journal and find five journal articles that use quantitative methods. Copy the section headings used in these articles. Compare the two lists. Do reports of field research seem to follow a particular pattern? If so, what is it? Answer the same questions for the quantitative articles.

7. Read the article by Matthews Hamabata that is included in the appendix. Discuss all the ways that he located himself in the research. What are the implications of his status characteristics on what he learned in the setting?

• • • • • • • • • • • • • • • • •

Appendix

Ethnographic Boundaries: Culture, Class, and Sexuality in Tokyo

Matthews Masayuki Hamabata

Yale University

ABSTRACT: For those engaged in participant-observation, the first few months in the field are usually extremely difficult. By taking a reflexive turn, however, the events recorded during entrée are invaluable for revealing the social and cultural dimensions of the new life a researcher creates for him- or herself. The following is an account of one researcher's attempt to enter a community in contemporary Tokyo. This account reveals the boundaries of culture, class, and sexuality between the researcher and the community. The complex set of highly personal ramifications resulting from crossing those boundaries is also discussed.

"Do the sociology," insisted Shulamit Reinharz, "as if your life depended on it" (Reinharz, 1979:363). And for my first (miserable) six months in Tokyo, it did. The issue at hand was not only one of applying social science, of observing and analyzing human behavior in a social and cultural context, in order to survive in the field (Reynolds and Farberow, 1976), but one of life itself, for I had none. To paraphrase Clifford Geertz (1973:412–413), I was without life, a specter of sorts, a ghost. And as such, I was often treated with deep suspicion in the guise of absolute indifference. A tremendous task, therefore, immediately confronted me: How was I to escape from ghosthood? How was I to create a totally new social identity for myself? For me

Many people have read various versions of this paper, but I would especially like to thank the following for taking the time to provide me with thought-provoking comments: Beverly Eliasoph, Steven Brint, Deborah Davis-Friedmann, Ezra Vogel, Robert J. Smith, Shulamit Reinharz, and Lee Rainwater. I am especially indebted to Dorinne Kondo, whose insights and warm support proved to be invaluable. Of course, all of the usual disclaimers apply. Address correspondence to: Department of Sociology, Yale University, New Haven, CT 06520.

that process was hardly the elegant Geertzian experience, whereby one somehow crosses "some moral or metaphysical shadow line" (Geertz, 1973:413). I became a person with an accompanying identity, with roles and obligations, by simply blundering about, by blundering across boundaries of culture, class, and sexuality.[1]

As a third-generation Japanese American, I had to immediately negotiate the boundary of culture: Was I inside or out? Well, the answer is quite simple: When I thought I was in, I was actually out; but when I acknowledged the fact that I was out, I was let in. Let's begin this story with how a Japanese cab driver in the city of Tokyo views the world. He (for it is almost always a he) is faced with a twelve-hour day, plying the heavy traffic and often narrow streets. Life on the streets of Tokyo is, therefore, full of minor irritations, not the least of which is someone who cannot give detailed instructions, for a written address means almost nothing in terms of finding the right house or apartment building. The ability to give detailed instructions is positively correlated with one's ability to speak Japanese; and since the cab driver, like many other Japanese, may "adhere to an eminently biological definition of Japaneseness" (Kondo, 1986: 76), in which race is inextricably tied to language and culture, he may choose to avoid *gaijin* (foreigners), the outsiders.[2]

The cab driver, therefore, views the *gaijin* as clearly outside his culture, even to the point where a *gaijin* could not be expected to learn to speak Japanese adequately.[3] I, of course, entered the field phenotypically Japanese, and although the culture was not new to me in many ways, the language certainly was. After studying it intensively for three years, I was good at it, but not perfect. All of this meant that the cab driver might happily pass by a *gaijin,* an outsider who couldn't be expected to give directions in Japanese, and stop for me: On the busy Tokyo street scene, my Japanese face alone made me an insider.

One particular cab ride sticks in my mind. I could pronounce the name of my destination perfectly, but I hadn't quite figured out how to say "right turn" and "left turn" in both the native Japanese manner and in the manner based on Chinese compounds. The brief exchange proceeded as follows:

I said: "Please take me to Minami Aoyama."
Cab driver: "It's a right turn at the intersection, isn't it?"
I replied: "Oh, no! *Please* turn right."

At which point, the car slowed almost to a crawl, and I could see the cab driver glare at me through his rearview mirror. He, no doubt, concluded that he had an exceedingly well-dressed moron in his back seat. This incident epitomizes my early experience in the field.

Dynastic households in the form of large-scale family enterprises were the subject of my study, and during those first few months of trying to gain entry into these enterprises, I began to move slowly but surely out of ghosthood. However, I suffered in that liminal period between ghosthood and personhood. As someone with a Japanese face but imperfect Japanese, I felt like and was treated as an incomplete human being. The Japanese were less than hospitable and often downright rude.

The source of many of my initial problems in the field stemmed from stubborn efforts to present myself as an insider, as a Japanese rather than as an American. I assumed that acting like an insider would accelerate my integration into Japanese culture.[4] I was sadly mistaken. When one possesses a Japanese face, the improper use of body and/or verbal language is quite jarring to the Japanese psyche, and so instead of being considered a rather talented foreigner who spent many years of hard work learning a difficult language, I was simply considered an undereducated Japanese at best and an incomplete Japanese at worst.

The trick for a Japanese American, I discovered, is to present oneself as an American—to shake hands and use English—when meeting people for the first time. The hospitable treatment normally accorded guests will then be forthcoming. Once having made one's entrée as a *gaijin*, however, it is possible to lose a bit of one's guest status as an "outsider" by switching into the Japanese mode. By switching, one is allowed to witness, and hear about, the nitty-gritty aspects of Japanese life. A sure sign of success is the following phrase, which precedes the most intimate revelation: "Well, of course, you are Japanese, and so you'll understand won't you?"[5] In other words, if one wisely manipulates one's duality as a Japanese American, one can partake of the best of both worlds—the graciousness accorded to guests and the intimacy reserved for insiders. If not, one is likely to experience the worst of both, that is, rude behavior and distance.

By blundering about, I learned to manipulate my dual identity, but unfortunately, I learned it at the expense of my original contacts. Through diplomatic circles, I had been introduced to members of one of the most elite of the large-scale family enterprises, one of international stature. Although they had tried to be kind to me during my first three or four months in the field, I got them just as confused as I was. Although I eventually learned to play my dual identity, I could not get rid of my early stigma of being that incomplete Japanese. As a result, the family members became increasingly polite and increasingly distant.

However, I had been seen with them at exclusive French restaurants and dinner parties in Tokyo, and so I somehow acquired some of their status. In the process of trying to pass me off to some other poor souls, my original contacts introduced me to more presidents of companies and their families. Much to my surprise, I became more and more a person in the eyes of this elite social circle. Suddenly, I found myself faced with the problem of crossing yet another boundary: class.

Now that I had become comfortable with my American and Japanese identities, I expected to be able to use my particular circumstance to enter into the lives of potential informants. By sharing some interesting tidbits about my life as a Japanese American, I hoped to be told about personal life experiences in return: a fair trade, I thought.[6] Again, I was wrong, for my frankness about my background touched upon an extremely sensitive issue in the lives of my growing circle of acquaintances and contacts. This circle was committed to the ideology that most Japanese are middle-class; yet they felt their lives were being encroached upon by ordinary people. One woman, for example, told me that she hated the arrival of festive days, for she would be forced to look at the tasteless silk *kimono* worn by ordinary women. The wearing of silk *kimono* should be reserved for women of good taste only, for women of position; yet this women would claim, if asked, that she was *futsuu* (ordinary, average).

I can still vividly recall the reactions I got when, in my naiveté, I mentioned that not only was I a third-generation Japanese American, but that I was also of Okinawan descent (an ethnic, island people subjugated by the mainland Japanese during the Tokugawa and Meiji periods). The shoulders would drop away from the head, as the back and neck straightened; the chin dropped; the lips pursed downward, as the following words were spoken: "A soo desu ka?" "Oh, is that right?" Then a polite smile would appear as my partner in conversation disappeared into the cocktail party.

The meaning of this reaction became absolutely clear when one woman told me that she was delighted to hear that I was a graduate student at Harvard. She was proud of the fact that Japanese were gifted enough to enter the best universities of the world; however, she made it clear that this wasn't always the case, for those who had emigrated to the United States three generations ago were the ignorant ones, the *heimin* (the plebian). This woman had assumed that my father was with a Japanese trading company in the United States, and that I had recently emigrated. The assumption: If one is at Harvard, one is of the upper class. How would I handle the fact that I wasn't?

Faced with a real fieldwork problem, with the fact of exclusivity, with the possibility of being shut out, I froze and offered very little information about myself. The tactic worked, and I learned an important code of behavior: *tatemae*. Japanese, unlike Americans, can easily accept duality in their lives; in other words, what appears on the surface may not necessarily correspond to the inner reality. Americans would tend to think that the inner reality was in some way "more real" and would, therefore, try to bring the inner to the surface. They would consider that to be honesty. Elite Japanese would say that was simply being ill-bred and ignorant, for the surface reality is just as real as the inner, private reality. The surface reality, the *tatemae*, exists for the smooth functioning of the surface world, the world of social relations, as opposed to the world of inner feelings (Kondo, 1982:45). As a general rule, one never looks beyond the *tatemae* in the social world. No one looked beyond my affiliation with Harvard University.

To *tatemae* one's circumstances often means to be passive, to simply accept others' assumptions about one's life. Unfortunately for me, total passivity was out of the question, for I was expected to act in the social world. To act in that world meant that one should have mastered the complex set of etiquette, from degrees of bowing to degrees of politeness in language. The thought terrified me, for I knew that I would be exposed: No matter how strong the resistance is to looking beyond the *tatemae*, even the Japanese cannot resist a peek, if one forces the situation. And during my first six months of fieldwork, I gave them more than a peek.

For a while, *zabuton* (floor cushions usually made of polished cotton) were the bane of my existence. I first encountered them at a formal, very crowded reception. The *zabuton*, used for sitting on *tatami* (straw mat) floors, were lined side by side; and since I needed to get from one end of the room to the other, they proved to be somewhat of an obstacle. I handled that situation by tromping across them to the horrified stares of the other guests. Not only had I violated rules of etiquette, but I had also tromped across deep codes of purity and impurity (Ohnuki-Tierney, 1984:21–50).

My instruction in proper behavior began with an informant showing me how to push my stockinged feet under the *zabuton* while *not* stepping on the silk embroidered edges of the *tatami* in the balancing act of getting across the room. My lessons in *zabuton* etiquette proceeded on to the timing of the acceptance of a *zabuton*, the appropriate approach and movement towards sitting on one, and the conditions under which one should or should not hop off the *zabuton* to perform *tetsuki* (kneeled floor bowing with hands placed directly in front of the body). As with any form of etiquette in Japan, the social context and the physical environment account for a high degree of *precise* variability in the rules. This made me feel as if I would never learn all of the proper forms of behavior. In fact, I had come to resign myself to the real possibility of being closed out of upper-class social circles.

The rules, however, slowly became ingrained in my behavior, and they even seemed manageable in social situations that were purely Japanese. Multicultural situations, however, turned out to be impossible. One evening I had been invited to a dinner hosted by a member of the Upper House of the Japanese Diet. Because of several European guests, the dinner was not the usual sex-segregated event. Wives were present and active participants in conversation. An elegant buffet was presented in the dining room, and dinner plates were brought into the living room for informal dining. It all seemed very comfortable, with a mix of French food and American manners.

Since I deferred to the others, I was the last to go through the buffet line and the last to enter the living room. As I was in the process of parking myself in the most convenient opening, I came to an instantaneous realization that I was about to invade the social space of the guest of honor, the present head of a household that once included a dramatic and politically powerful prince in the early Showa period. However, I had no time to change my course of action, and as I proceeded to sit down, a look of resigned disbelief crossed everyone's face.

In those terrifying few seconds, I belatedly drew in my mind a figure of standard seating arrangements. Mr. Bun Nakajima of the Japan Travel Bureau provides us with a more accurate, basic picture (Nakajima, 1957:17).[7] In Figure 1, the numbers show the order of seating according to rank and/or status as a guest.

By taking a place to the left of the "original" guest of honor, I compounded my error by usurping his position of being the highest status male in the group. Again, I blundered into another impossible situation because of my Japanese American identity. While all the other foreign guests were assigned "guides," I was left to my own inadequate devices since I was thought to be essentially Japanese.

Figure 1

Order of Seating According to Rank and/or Status as a Guest

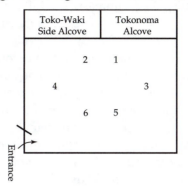

Meanwhile, I was under the impression that the situation called for essentially American patterns of behavior!

Not knowing what to do with the elegant and clearly uncomfortable guest of honor, who was forced to share his loveseat with me, I blurted out in English, "I see you have a lot of watercress piled on your plate. I love the stuff myself." He smiled and said that he had acquired a taste for it while he was a student at the London School of Economics. The sigh of relief was almost audible. Another trick learned: Use English in tight spots. This event proved to be a watershed of sorts, for it brought me right into elite social circles: The richer one is, the more social codes one can break, especially if it is done with a bit of panache. And panache is often equated with having a Japanese face and speaking perfect English.

Figure 2

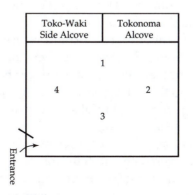

The boundaries of culture and class were to be fully expected. I was, however, completely taken by surprise when I ran into the boundary of sexuality. As an unmarried adult male, I was considered to be sexually available and, therefore, a threat. That threat was handled in a variety of ways: Young husbands were cool to me; daughters were nervous in my company; everyone fretted. In the fifth month of fieldwork, my informants had begun to like and trust me, but as a sexually available male, it became more and more difficult for them to continue their relationships with me, and so one of them took it upon herself to solve the problem.

Mrs. Nishimura, a young wife of about thirty-one years of age, invited me to join her for tea at 4:00. When I arrived, she informed me that several of her friends would drop by that afternoon. At 4:10, a woman with a degree in Romance languages from the Tokyo Foreign Languages University came by; she excused herself at about 4:45. At 5:00, a graduate student in German history at Tokyo University came by; she stayed until 5:30. The last guest, also female, was an intern at the Women's Medical University Hospital.

Mrs. Nishimura: "Weren't they nice?"

"Yes, they were."

Mrs. Nishimura: "And they're all so intelligent."

"Yes, they seem to be."

Mrs. Nishimura: "But these successful career women always have problems with marriage. It's too bad. They're all almost thirty, and if they don't get married soon, it will be even more difficult."

Terror struck my heart, and I beat a hasty retreat, saying that I had a dinner engagement.

I thought that I had made a clean getaway. Mrs. Nishimura, however, was not about to give up her chance to *endan o tsukuru*, to make a marriage proposal, and so she called me the next day, suggesting that we lunch at the Imperial Hotel. I picked away at my chicken salad, as she tried to shame me into marriage.

"Who are you to think that you could refuse to consider my friends? They're all from good families. Do you think that your family is better? Furthermore, any man of your age should be married. How embarrassing to think that you won't even consider marriage. Finally, you are being *fukoo*, undutiful to your parents," she scolded, her face wrinkled with annoyance.

The pressure was on, and in fact, I began to feel badly about my unmarried status. Overcome with cultural confusion, I began to babble on nervously in Japanese, apologizing: "Yes, I know that I should get married soon. Of course, a Japanese wife would be perfect. But I would make an inadequate husband given my circum-stances. I move about the world too much. My wife would suffer. My children would suffer. It would be a bad marriage. And so even my parents would suffer. I would be even more *fukoo*, unfilial, if I were to marry."

Well, that convinced her. I won her over on her own terms. It was a question of what would be more unfilial: to marry or not to marry. I left the Imperial Hotel and wandered aimlessly about the Ginza, reeling from the experience of becoming totally identified with the *fukoo mono*, the unfilial child, among the Japanese elite. The bound-ary of sexuality appeared before me with great clarity. If I didn't cross it, I would spend my remaining months in the field, feeling dizzy with shame and having all of my informants either trying to arrange marriages for me or trying to avoid me. As a sexually avail-able male, I became my own biggest fieldwork problem.[8]

From that point onward, I found myself becoming increasingly naive about worldly matters. When my informants would ask me about the change in sexual mores among young Americans, for ex-ample, I feigned complete ignorance. My status as a student also came increasingly to the forefront; the image of the *gakusei-san* (stu-dent), even more than in the United States, is one of immaturity, and it is the image that I cultivated. In Japan, patterns of behavior that separate the men from the boys are quite clear-cut, and I found my-self adopting boyish language and tastes. I referred to myself only as *boku*, which is a form of the pronoun "I." A male could refer to him-self in the more formal *watakushi* or the informal, extremely mascu-line *ore*, but I used the boyish *boku*. I, as *boku*, also developed a keen liking for Japanese sweets, French pastry, and Baskin-Robbins ice cream. Children love sweets in Japan, but boys at puberty learn to detest cakes and candies; and as men, they take to smoking ciga-rettes and drinking scotch.

The ploy may have been simple, but it worked. By becoming a boy, I pulled myself out of the sexual market: no longer was I consid-ered a threat. It was, at times, difficult to accept my identity as a sexually and socially immature male, and I still remember the shock I felt when one of my married female informants turned to me at a specialty food store in the Imperial Hotel Arcade and asked, *"Boku wa nani ka hoshii?"* By addressing me with the pronoun *boku* instead of my family name, she was inferring a very high degree of familiar-ity, indeed of intimacy. However, because of the age difference of about twenty years and her married status, it was an intimacy that was hierarchical in nature; in fact, an *oneesan* (older sister) would address a younger brother with *boku*. My informant, therefore, was asking the Japanese equivalent of "Does the little boy want something?"[9] It was, to say the least, both irritating and embarrassing, but it was a mark of success: I seemed to have reversed the biological and social processes of maturing.[10]

We began this episode of my life in Japan, of crossing boundaries, with a cab ride; let's continue with another. Fourteen very long months had gone by, and I found myself in yet another taxi, giving directions to the driver for the quickest route to Roppongi. My Japanese had been perfect, if perhaps a bit too polite, but I apologized for its imperfection. The cab driver was startled to find out that I had been born in the United States, and his curiosity was piqued. What was I doing in Japan? What number son was I? Was California rice really as good as Japanese rice? Along with my preferences for rice, he found out that I was still a *gakusei-san* (a student), who was born the third son in a family of five siblings. At this point, he launched into a diatribe against the present generation of Japanese youth, simultaneously assuring me that *mukoo no nihonjin* (the Japanese "over there," abroad) maintained the traditions of Meiji Japan, and that I was an example of that culture, an example of a *shit-suke no ii* (a well-disciplined) Japanese.

The cab driver's comments confirmed that the creation of my new social identity, my *tatemae*, my Tokyo mask, had become complete.[11] As a *gakusei-san*, I was a socially immature male, not quite ready for marriage. Furthermore, I was more Japanese than American; in fact, I was a Japanese of the old-fashioned, Meiji kind. After dropping me off at Roppongi Crossing, the taxi sped off, leaving me with thoughts about my Tokyo identity and the task of receiving yet another forty thousand yen (approximately U.S. $200) gift from Mrs. Tani.

In my seven pieces of luggage that I brought with me to the field were a number of Harvard University souvenirs: ashtrays, T-shirts and the like. I had been forewarned that gift-giving was a crucial aspect of social life in Japan, and that I should be prepared. Those gifts, however, sat in their boxes for several months; that was, unfortunately, indicative of my life as a ghost. To become a person, one needs an identity and a role. We have seen how I came to create a social identity for myself through interaction with Japanese informants. The roles that came to be established for me also came through interaction with others, and gift-giving turned out to be a defining dimension of that interaction.

Gift-giving in Japan, to say the least, is complex. The anthropologist Harumi Befu counted at least thirty-five different terms for gifts, ranging from "introductory good will gift" to "funerary gift" (Morsbach 1977:99), and the items themselves range from cash to seasoned laver (Nakajima, 1957:78–79). Of course, my Harvard souvenirs turned out to be clearly, and sadly, inadequate.

In my early period of ghosthood, I exchanged gifts only three or four times a month.[12] The initial outlay of about U.S. 100 dollars at the Harvard Cooperative Society lasted for a little over three months. During my last eight months in the field, I exchanged gifts three or four times a week and easily spent from U.S. 100 dollars to U.S. 250 dollars a month in outgoing gifts.

The increasing frequency and monetary value of the gift exchanges in which I participated are measures of my increasing involvement in tightly knit groups and of my roles within these groups becoming more clearly defined. I found myself increasingly embedded in face-to-face relationships with specific persons whose roles were tied to specific settings, and I must agree with Helmut Morsbach, who wrote, "to keep these relationships going smoothly requires an acute awareness of reciprocal obligations and their appropriate fulfillment. These often function at the nonverbal level, and are mainly of a highly ritualized nature. Gift exchange is an excellent example" (Morsbach, 1977:99).

By participating in particular settings of gift exchange, a person not only reaffirms his or her connectedness to others but also comes to an understanding of his or her role, as it comes to be defined through interaction with specified others. That role takes shape as the process of gift exchange gives concrete meaning to three defining concepts in Japanese social relationships: *on*, *giri*, and *ninjoo*. An *on* relationship arises when one receives some resource from an *on*-giver that one, as an *on*-receiver, does not have. There is an expectation that this *on* would be repaid. However, since one cannot repay in kind (for one never had the desired resource from the very beginning of the exchange), the resource that is dispensed in repayment is qualitatively different and noncomparable; therefore, one, in essence, can never repay *on*, no matter how hard one tries. As an *on*-receiver, one is in a hierarchical relationship in which one is the subordinate.

Giri, like *on*, is a concept based on social obligations; however, it is not necessarily one that is hierarchical in nature. It can occur in relationships that are basically egalitarian. A good person, furthermore, is *giri-gatai*, that is, someone who recognizes and observes moral and ethical codes of conduct. "In short, *giri* is the normative force that attempts to maintain social institutions in a smooth-running condition, irrespective of how an individual might feel about

the social order or about other persons with whom he might interact" (Befu, 1971:169).

In sharp contrast to *giri* is the concept of *ninjoo*, the world of personal feelings. It may, in fact, be possible for personal inclinations to
be in opposition to *giri*, to the social and the moral. This situation is,
of course, the stuff of great Japanese tragedies (Befu, 1971:170). In
contradistinction to this dilemma is the happy coming together of
ninjoo with *giri* and/or *on*.

As a crucial form of social interaction in Japan, Morsbach pointed
out that gift-giving also falls within the realm of those three concepts. In fact, there are *on* gifts, *giri* gifts, and *ninjoo* gifts (Morsbach,
1977:100–101). By embodying those ideal-typical forms of social relationships, gift-giving shapes role expectations. Gift-giving is a perfect example of the Geertzian concept of a cultural system serving as
a *model of* and a *model for* social behavior (Geertz, 1968:9); it both reflects and shapes human society. It is, therefore, through gift exchange that the individual and his or her significant others come to
develop and modify their roles vis-à-vis each other. My first serious
encounter with gift exchange came three and a half months into my
fieldwork experience.

By February of 1980, I had developed a close friendship with
Mrs. Tani and her only daughter, Sanae. We had been meeting frequently to discuss the prospect of an American college education for
Sanae, and in fact, I had helped Sanae with her applications to
Princeton, Columbia, Stanford, and other universities. By mid-Feb-
ruary all of the applications had been completed, and the three of us
gathered to celebrate and to talk about what college life in the
United States would be like for Sanae. Mrs. Tani's habitually ex-
travagant tastes dictated that we meet at one of the small but terri-
bly expensive bistros that dot Roppongi, a major entertainment district in Tokyo.

Feeling a little lonely and lost in the city, I looked forward to
these outings with Sanae and her mother, who seemed to attract attention and pleasant company wherever we went. This particular
evening was not any different from all of the others: interesting food
and conversation. Just as we were about to part company, Mrs. Tani
handed me a small, carefully wrapped box and a card, saying that
she was embarrassed at presenting me with something so inadequate in return for all of the help I had given Sanae. "It's nothing,"
she claimed in English.

On the subway ride home, I discovered that I had received a
Valentine's Day card and a box of chocolates. It was a small present,

but I was touched. They had remembered that it was Valentine's Day, an event which I had ignored in the United States, but for some odd reason, it had taken on some significance now that I was separated from American rites and rituals. To say the least, I had been pleased to find that Mrs. Tani and Sanae had become my friends.

Delighted with my gift, I opened the box at home with the intention of sharing the chocolates with my roommate, and out fell 50,000 yen (about 250 U.S. dollars) in five crisp, 10,000-yen bills. I was, at once, shocked, insulted, and hurt. I ranted and raved: "Who do the Tanis think they are? They can't buy me or my services!" My instincts told me to return the money as soon as possible, but the social scientist in me made me make some phone calls first.

I called an American anthropologist, who called her informants for advice. I also called my own Japanese informants. The outcome of it all was that while my American friends advised me to return the money, the Japanese asked very specific questions: How did my relationship with the Tanis begin? What did I do for them? What did they do for me? Could I make a guesstimation about their financial status? How was the money presented? When was the presentation made? And so on.

The calculations were made as follows: (1) Since the Tanis had initiated the relationship and had acquired some resource from me that they did not possess, that is, knowledge about the American educational system, they were in an *on* relationship with me, and I was the *on*-giver; therefore, the gift of money and chocolates was a return *on*-gift; (2) because the gift was presented after I had completed my favor for them; it could definitely *not* be considered a bribe, but a true gift of appreciation, a true gift of return *on*; (3) because of their immense wealth, 50,000 yen was a small token, relatively speaking; (4) since the money was accompanied by a gift that was personally selected by the Tanis for an occasion that was particularly meaningful to me, it also embodied *ninjoo*, personal feelings; the *on*, therefore, was not mere obligation but also backed with inner feelings; the gift was a combination *on/ninjoo* presentation; (5) finally, the gift was a sign that the Tanis needed me in some way, and if I were to discontinue the relationship because of that, I would not be operating in the Japanese mode, for the Japanese believe that one always has to depend upon face-to-face relationships with specific individuals in order to survive in the world.

Given that interpretation, I could not have, in good conscience, returned the money, for it would have been taken as a slap in the face, and in fact, I had originally wanted to do just that: Return an insult for an insult. However, with the help of Japanese informants, I came to the realization that the role that was developing for me in my relationship with the Tanis was that of *on*-giver, and that there was an expectation of magnanimity, of continuing that relationship of dependence. The gift, therefore, was an indication of a developing role and of developing role expectations.

I, however, did not feel as if too many sacrifices were made on my part, in terms of providing a bit of college counseling for Sanae, but I was afraid of my role as *on*-giver developing into something more than I could manage. In other words, I had nightmares of Sanae finally attending an American university, and that I would be expected to be responsible for her welfare, *in loco parentis*. Given these realistic fears and concerns, I needed to modify the Tanis's role expectations vis-à-vis myself, and this could be accomplished through a return gift.

What surprised me the most about making a return gift is the exact monetary calculation made; that is, since a gift embodies ideal-typical relationships, a cost evaluation of the gift implies that there is a cost evaluation of those relationships. In fact, I was told that given my concerns, I should make a return gift that would leave me 25,000 yen ahead: The Tanis would then feel free to ask favors of me, to continue their dependence on me, yet I would be clearly setting limits on their expectations of me as an *on*-giver. Morsbach noted that the "ideal value" of a gift is not divorced from its "monetary value," and that it would be premature to conclude from this that the Japanese gift-giving customs must necessarily be devoid of feeling; it is simply that attempts at balancing obligations *exactly* are so much more important, and knowing the price of the gift allows one to do this (Morsbach, 1977:100–101). In my case, it was not so much the balancing of obligations but the *modifying* of them that needed to be calculated *exactly*.

"When making a gift of flowers, you should go to Goto-san's place." That's the advice I was given, and so in making my return gift, I went to Goto Florists in Roppongi and selected orchids, fifteen blossoms at 2,000 yen (about 10 U.S. dollars) a piece. I enclosed a note in English saying that I truly enjoyed the Tanis's friendship, but that they were much too kind. Our relationship still continues, but my role as *on*-giver has been delimited: I sometimes get long-distance telephone calls from Sanae, now at an Ivy League university, who asks about course selections and the like; those calls are immediately followed by ones from Mrs. Tani who thanks me profusely, apologizes for her daughter's selfishness, and asks me to dine with them again in Tokyo or New York

It took nine months of sheer anxiety, but through a complex and delicate kind of involvement with many patient and a few not-so-patient Japanese, my new social identity began to emerge, and as I began to discover that I had a few important resources that were not easily available to my informants, my role in their lives began to take the broad shape of *on*-giver. I became an English language tutor for the children, a college counselor, and a friend and personal adviser to several *okusama*, wives. As my social identity and my roles coalesced, I crossed that final boundary between ghosthood and personhood.

At this very moment, however, the anxious billowing of cigarette smoke belies the comfort I take in sitting in my office, surrounded by my typewriter and piles of unread manuscripts, writing about my experiences in the field, thinking that Japan is very, very far away, trying to convince myself that I have left the "other me" back there, that he died when I returned to the United States. Leaving the field is, indeed, problematic not only because of the kinds of commitment and levels of intimacy that one establishes with one's informants (Crapanzano, 1980; Maines et al., 1980; Roadburg, 1980), but also because of the commitment one has to the other person one has become in the field. That other person, the "other me," cannot be left behind.

Without a doubt, I was resocialized (Wax, 1971:3–20) in Tokyo, gaining a new and different sense of myself and the world, a sense that I have deeply internalized (Reinharz, 1979:373–374). One could say that the experience changed me in fundamental ways (Emerson, 1981). But I do not live comfortably with that change. The very writing of this piece is symptomatic of that uneasy state of being.

By writing, by giving a narrative structure to the events experienced in the field, by telling stories, I am, on one level of interpretation, trying to gain some cognitive and affective distance on, as well as some understanding of, my life (and humiliation) in the field (Daniels 1983:208). Writing is, in fact, tied to my need to "exorcise" the experience of fieldwork (Crapanzano, 1977). But perhaps, at another level of interpretation, I may have been compelled to write in order to "exorcise" the "other me," thereby reconstituting myself (Kondo, 1986) in ways somehow more familiar, in ways seemingly more real and authentic

My writing and telling of stories, however, have not served their purpose. By giving the "other me" a mere textual existence, I had hoped to drain him of blood,[13] which I may have done; but, para-doxically, I also kept him alive. With the writing of every episode, with its rereading and retelling, he reappears. He returns to inform my present and my past, giving my world additional, albeit un-wanted, meaning. In his textuality, without flesh, without blood, he lives to judge me and my life. He tells me that once, long ago in To-kyo, as a Japanese person, I was, indeed, a better human being. Back then, I knew right from wrong. Right now, I flout all of the moral and ethical codes of conduct, which once shaped my entire exist-ence, codes that I once believed were, and should continue to know are, just.

I may have wanted the "other me" to die when I left the field, but he simply refused to stop existing.

He haunts me still.

NOTES

1. By "blundering," I actually mean that hypotheses about human behav-ior in Japanese society, derived from my social scientific observations, were actually tested in the very actions that I took to establish myself as a person in a community (Reinharz, 1979:364); unfortunately, those hy-potheses often proved to be dead wrong.

2. See Nakane (1970:20) for further explications of the inside/outside dis-tinction in Japanese society. This inside/outside dichotomy and the at-titudes that are embedded within it are ideographically represented in the word *gaijin*, which is made up of the characters for "outside" and "person."

3. This cultural construct of outside status is coupled with the reality of 1400 years of racial homogeneity in the Japanese archipelago (Morsbach, 1973:262).

4. Because of my Japanese face, there was an arrogant assumption on my part that the kind of "familiar distance" (Crapanzano, 1980:12) often necessary for the gathering of information had already been estab-lished, even before I entered the field. In other words, I thought that I would be familiar enough to the Japanese, so that they would feel free enough to speak about things that a "true" foreigner would not be ex-pected to understand, and I also thought that as an American national, I would be distant enough to provide neutral space, in which that spe-cial kind of frankness in ethnographic discourse could appear. In retro-spect, I should have heeded Rosalie Wax's warning: "Perhaps the most egregious error that a fieldworker can commit is to assume that he can win the immediate regard of his hosts by telling them that he wants to 'become one of them' or by implying, by word or act, that the fact that they tolerate his presence means that he *is* one of them" (Wax, 1971:47).

5. There are three equally valid interpretations of this phrase and its meaning in the interactions between myself and my informants in the

early phases of fieldwork. The first is that my informants were trying to neutralize any critical judgments that I as a foreigner, may have had about their lives. They were trying to elicit my support and sympathy (Pollner and Emerson, 1983:241). And to a large extent, they were successful, for I had desperately wanted to be recognized as a Japanese; thus, that phrase of inclusion elicited feelings of sympathy, as well as those of warmth (Kondo 1986:77–78) and security, which arise from the sense of belonging (at last!). Because feelings of warmth and security were elicited, this phrase was also used on the part of my informants as a reward for proper behavior or thought. It is clear that we were all engaged in my resocialization, an essential process in coming to understand the culture in which I was to become immersed (Wax, 1971:3–20). Resocialization, however, is only the second way of setting that phrase of inclusion in a socio-cultural context and interpreting its meaning. The third, and final, way has to do with the kind of *angst* that arises between the fieldworker and his or her informants. As Vincent Crapanzano pointed out, the ethnographic process brings about changes in the consciousness on the part of those investigated, as well as those who do the investigating (Crapanzano, 1980:11). And as the fieldworker and his or her informants become increasingly intimate, there comes a realization that many of the essential aspects of life, even the concept of "person," can no longer be taken for granted. Recognizing that there are alternative and equally satisfying ways of constituting reality can throw everyone involved in the ethnographic process into an ontological, as well as epistemological, crisis (Crapanzano, 1977). Because I was physically Japanese, yet culturally American, I posed a special threat to my informants, a threat to their personal identities (Kondo, 1986:76), their sense of the world and the way it was constituted. The epistemological crisis, however, was staved off by my informants, for they realized my situation of dependence and, thus, their position of power over me. They simply proceeded to make me more "wholly" Japanese and, therefore, less threatening, through the process of resocialization. And, of course, I colluded in that process (Kondo 1986:76–78; Pollner and Emerson, 1983).

6. On trading information among informants, see Daniels (1983;1967) and Rabinow (1977).

7. I have added the place of entrance, which was lacking in the original drawing.

8. Although sexual intimacy may be treated simply as a fact of the human condition that finds expression in the field (Rabinow, 1977), or as a problem of informants desiring greater intimacy with the fieldworker (Pollner and Emerson, 1983 240–242), I found it to be the ultimate threat to my identity. In a society such as Japan, where the institution of marriage remains unquestioned, where marriage is practically universal (Soorifu, 1984:3–7; Cornell, 1984), and where it is considered essential to one's identity as an adult (Hamabata, 1983: 188–267), marriage was just one more step in the process of my resocialization. Given that I had already "traded in" so much of my identity as an American, I simply could not trade in my sexuality, not for some sense of ethical responsibility to

science and the people that I studied but for the very mundane sense of psychological survival.

9. Another variation in the use of the personal pronoun *boku:* If the female is of the same age as the male, whom she addresses as *boku,* it implies a certain degree of possessiveness, as well as intimacy. The relationship, therefore, would almost always be defined as romantic.

10. In downplaying my sexuality, Shulamit Reinharz asked if this did not bring me ostracism and/or ridicule (personal communication, July 1985); and, indeed, it did. Because I was not considered a mature adult, a "real man," as it were, by adult Japanese males, I was "left" in the company of women, who treated me as either a son or a younger brother. This left me open to ridicule by males, culminating in their ostracism. As a result, my research began to focus, more and more, on the lives of women.

11. See Berreman (1973) on masking as impression management in the field.

12. In 1972 Harumi Befu collected data on gift-giving events in 76 households, and over a period of 6.9 months, households averaged 13.2 incoming gifts and 10.2 outgoing gifts per month (Morsbach, 1977:100).

13. See Kondo (1986) for an extremely insightful analysis of writing and symbolic violence.

REFERENCES

Befu, Harumi
    1971 *Japan: An Anthropological Introduction.* San Francisco: Chandler Publishing Company.

Berreman, Gerald D.
    1973 "Behind many masks: Ethnography and impression management in a Himalayan village." Pp. 268–312 in Donald Warwick and Samuel Osherson (eds.), *Comparative Research Methods.* Englewood Cliffs: Prentice-Hall.

Cornell, Laurel
    1984 "Why are there no spinsters in Japan?" *Journal of Family History* 9:326–339.

Crapanzano, Vincent
    1977 "On the writing of ethnography." *Dialectical Anthropology* 2:69–73.
    1980 *Tuhami: Portrait of a Moroccan.* Chicago: University of Chicago Press.

Daniels, Arlene Kaplan
    1967 "The low-caste stranger in social research." Pp. 267–296 in Gideon Sjoberg (ed.), *Ethics Politics and Social Research.* Cambridge: Schenkman.
    1983 "Self-deception and self-discovery in fieldwork." *Qualitative Sociology* 6:195–214.

Emerson, Robert M.
    1981 "Observational field work." *Annual Review of Sociology* 7:351–378.

Geertz, Clifford'
1968 "Religion as a cultural system." Pp. 1–46 in M. Banton (ed.), *Anthropological Approaches to the Study of Religion*. London: Tavistock.
1973 "Deep play: Notes on the Balinese cockfight." Pp. 412–453 in *The Interpretation of Cultures*. New York: Basic Books.

Hamabata, Matthews M.
1983 From Household to Enterprise. Unpublished doctoral dissertation, Department of Sociology, Harvard University, Cambridge, Massachusetts.

Kondo, Dorinne
1982 Work, Family and Self. Unpublished doctoral dissertation, Department of Anthropology, Harvard University, Cambridge, Massachusetts.
1986 "Dissolution and reconstitution of self: Implications for anthropological epistemology." *Cultural Anthropology* 1:74–88.

Maines, David, William Shaffir and Allan Turowitz
1980 "Leaving the field in ethnographic research: Reflections on the entrance-exit hypothesis." Pp. 261–281 in William Shaffir, et al. (eds.), *Fieldwork Experience: Qualitative Approaches to Social Research*. New York: St. Martin's Press.

Morsbach, Helmut
1973 "Aspects of nonverbal communication in Japan." *The Journal of Nervous and Mental Disease* 157:262–277.
1977 "The psychological importance of ritualized gift exchange in modern Japan." Pp. 98–113 in *Annals, New York Academy of Sciences: Anthropology and the Climate of Opinion*. New York: New York Academy Sciences.

Nakajima, Bun
1957 *Japanese Etiquette*. Tokyo: Toppan Printing Company.

Nakane, Chie
1970 *Japanese Society*. Berkeley: University of California Press.

Ohnuki-Tierney, Emiko
1984 *Illness and Culture in Contemporary Japan*. Cambridge: Cambridge University Press.

Pollner, Melvin and Robert Emerson
1983 "The dynamics of inclusion and distance in fieldwork relations." Pp. 235–252 in Robert Emerson (ed.), *Contemporary Field Research*. Boston: Little, Brown.

Rabinow, Paul
1977 *Reflections on Fieldwork in Morocco*. Berkeley: University of California Press.

Reinharz, Shulamit
1979 *On Becoming a Social Scientist*. San Francisco: Jossey-Bass

Reynolds, D. K. and N. L. Farberow
1976 *Suicide: Inside and out*. Berkeley: University of California Press.

Roadburg, Allan
1980 "Breaking relationships with research subjects: Some problems

and suggestions." Pp. 281–291 in William Shaffir et al. (eds.), *Fieldwork Experience: Qualitative Approaches to Social Research.* New York: St. Martin's Press.

Soorifu Koohoo Shitsu
   1984 *Seron Choosa 16* (October).

Wax, Rosalie
   1971 *Doing Fieldwork: Warnings and Advice.* Chicago: University of Chicago Press.

References

Adler, Patricia. (1985). *Wheeling and dealing*. New York: Columbia University Press.

Adler, Patricia A., and Adler, Peter. (1994). Shifts and oscillations in deviant careers: The case of upper-level drug dealers and smugglers. In Patricia Adler and Peter Adler (Eds.), *Constructions of deviance: Social power, context, and interaction* (pp. 560–586). Belmont, CA: Wadsworth.

American Sociological Association. (1994). *Code of ethics*. Washington DC: Author.

Atkinson, Paul, and Hammersley, Martyn. (1994). Ethnography and participant observations. In Norman K. Denzin and Yvonna S. Lincoln (Eds.), *Handbook of qualitative research* (pp. 248-261). Thousand Oaks, CA: Sage.

Baber, Kristine, and Allen, Katherine. (1992). *Women and families: Feminist reconstructions*. New York: The Guilford Press.

Bailey, Brooke. (1994). *The remarkable lives of 100 women healers and scientists*. Holbrook. MA: Bob Adams, Inc.

Bailey, Kenneth D. (1978). *Methods of social research*. New York: The Free Press.

Berger, Peter L., and Luckman, Thomas. (1967). *The social construction of reality*. New York: Doubleday-Anchor.

Blum, Linda, and Vandewater, Elizabeth. (1993). Mothers construct fathers: Destablized patriarchy in La Leche League. *Qualitative Sociology, 16*, 3–22.

Buckholdt, R. D., and Gubrium, J. F. (1979). *Caretakers: Treating emotionally disturbed children*. Beverly Hills: Sage.

Bulmer, M. (1982). *Social research ethics*. London: Macmillan.

Burgess, Robert G. (1991). Sponsors, gatekeepers, members, and friends: Access in educational settings." In William B. Shaffir and Robert A. Stebbins (Eds.), *Experiencing fieldwork: An inside view of qualitative research* (pp. 43–52). New York: St. Martin's Press.

Chagnon, Napoleon. (1968). *Yanomamo: The fierce people*. New York: Holt, Rinehard and Winston.

Crystal, S. (1984). Homeless men and homeless women: The gender gap. *Urban and Social Change Review, 17*, 2–6.

Dean, John P., Eichhorn, Robert L., and Dean, Lois R. (1969). Establishing field relations. In George J. McCall and J. L. Simmons (Eds.), *Issues in participant observation: A text and reader*. Reading, MA: Addison-Wesley.

Denzin, Norman K. (1994). The art and politics of interpretation. In Norman K. Denzin and Yvonna S. Lincoln (Eds.), *Handbook of qualitative research* (pp. 500–515). Thousand Oaks, CA: Sage.

Denzin, Norman K., and Lincoln, Yvonna S. (Eds.). (1994). *Handbook of qualitative research*. Thousand Oaks, CA: Sage.

Douglas, Jack. (1979). Living morality versus bureaucratic fiat. In C. B. Klockars and F. W. O'Connor (Eds.), *Deviance and decency* (pp. 13–33). Beverly Hills: Sage.

Downey, Gary. (1986). Ideology and the clamshell identity: Organizational dilemmas in the anti–nuclear power movement. *Social Problems, 33,* 357–373.

Eco-warriors. (1990, Nov. 7). *New York Times.*

Emerson, Robert. (1988). *Contemporary field research: A collection of readings*. Prospect Heights, IL: Waveland Press.

Ferron (Singer). (1980). Ain't life a brook. *Testimony*. (Recording). Oakland, CA: Redwood Records.

Fetterman, David. (1982). Ethnography in educational research: The dynamics of diffusion. *Educational Researcher, 11,* 17–29.

Fetterman, David. (1989). *Ethnography: Step by step*. Newbury Park, CA: Sage.

Fielder, Judith. (1978). *Field research: A manual for logistics and management of scientific studies in natural settings*. San Francisco: Jossey-Bass.

Fontana, Andrea, and Frey, James. (1994). Interviewing: The art of science. In Norman K. Denzin and Yvonna S. Lincoln (Eds.), *Handbook of Qualitative Research* (pp. 361–376). Thousand Oaks, CA: Sage.

Fox, Kathryn. (1994). Real punks and pretenders: The social organization of a counterculture. In Patricia Adler and Peter Adler (Eds.), *Constructions of deviance: Social power, context, and interaction* (pp. 373–388). Belmont, CA: Wadsworth.

Fuhrman, Ellsworth. (in press). *Transformation of self and society: On the moral foundation of modern (and postmodern) theory*. Dix Hill, NY: General Hall, Inc.

Galliher, J. F. (1982). The protection of human subjects: A re-examination of the professional code of ethics. In M. Bulmer (Ed.), *Social research ethics* (pp. 152–165). London: Macmillan.

Gans, H. J. (1962). *The urban villagers: Group and class in the life of Italian-Americans*. New York: Free Press.

Geertz, Clifford. (1973). *The interpretation of cultures*. New York: Basic Books.

Geertz, Clifford. (1979). From the native's point of view: On the nature of anthropological understanding. In Paul Rabinow and William Sullivan (Eds.), *Interpretive social science: A reader* (pp. 225–242). Berkeley: University of California Press.

Glaser, Barney, and Strauss, Anselm. (1967). *The discovery of grounded theory*. Chicago: Aldine.

Gold, Raymond. (1969). Roles in sociological field observation. In G. J. McCall and J. L. Simmons (Eds.), *Issues in participant observation* (pp. 30–38). Reading, MA: Addison-Wesley.

Golde, Peggy. (1986). Odyssey of encounter. In Peggy Golde (Ed.), *Women in the field: Anthropological experiences* (pp. 67–93). Berkeley: University of California Press.

Goode, Erich, and Preissler, Joanne. (1990). The fat admirer. In Clifton D. Bryant (Ed.), *Deviant behavior: Readings in the sociology of norm violations* (pp. 325–437). New York: Hemisphere.

Gubrium, Jaber. (1986). *Oldtimers and Alzheimer's: The descriptive organization of senility.* Greenwich, CT: JAI.

Gurnery, Joan. (1982). Not one of the guys: The female researcher in a male-dominated setting. *Qualitative Sociology, 8,* 42–62.

Harari, Herber, Harari, Oren, and White, Robert V. (1985). The reaction to rape by American bystanders. *Journal of Social Psychology, 125,* 653, 658.

Hopper, Columbus B., and Moore, Johnny. (1994). Women in outlaw motorcycle gangs. In Patricia A. Adler and Peter Adler (Eds.), *Constructions of deviance: Social power, context, and interaction* (pp. 389–401). Belmont, CA: Wadsworth.

Humphreys, Laud. (1970). *Tearoom trade: Impersonal sex in public places.* New York: Aldine de Gruter.

Hunt, Jennifer. (1984). The development of rapport through the negotiation of gender in fieldwork among the police. *Human Organization, 43,* 283–296.

Ianni, Francis. (1972). *A family business.* New York: Russell Sage.

Ianni, Francis. (1974). *Black Mafia: Ethnic succession in organized crime.* New York: Simon & Schuster.

Johnson, J. M. (1975). *Doing field research.* London: Free Press.

Johnson, Norris. (1986). Ethnographic research and rites of incorporation: A sex and gender-based comparison. In T. L. Whitehead and M. E. Conaway (Eds.), *Self, sex and gender in cross-cultural fieldwork* (pp. 164–181). Urbana: University of Illinois Press.

Jorgensen, Danny. (1989). *Participant observation: A methodology for human studies.* Newbury Park, CA: Sage.

Junker, Buford. (1960). *Field work.* Chicago: University of Chicago Press.

Karp, David. (1994). Illness ambiguity and the search for meaning: A case study of a self-help group for affective disorders. In Patricia Adler and Peter Adler (Eds.), *Constructions of deviance: Social power, context, and interaction* (pp. 338–349). Belmont, CA: Wadsworth.

Kincheloe, Joe, and McLaren, Peter L. (1994). Rethinking critical theory and qualitative research. In Norman K. Denzin and Yvonna S. Lincoln (Eds.), *Handbook of qualitative research* (pp. 138–257). Thousand Oaks, CA: Sage.

Klein, Alan. (1994). Managing deviance: Hustling, homophobia, and the bodybuilding subculture. In Patricia Adler and Peter Adler (Eds.), *Constructions of deviance: Social power, context, and interaction* (pp. 529–544). Belmont, CA: Wadsworth.

Kleinman, Sherry. (1980). Learning the ropes as fieldwork analysis. In W. B. Shaffir, R. A. Stebbins, and A. Turowetz (Eds.), *Fieldwork experience* (pp. 171–183). New York: St. Martin's Press.

Klockars, Carl. (1974). *The professional fence.* New York: Free Press.

Liebow, Elliot (1967). *Talley's corner.* Boston: Little, Brown

Liebow, Elliot. (1994). *Tell them who I am: The lives of homeless women.* New York: The Free Press.

Livingston, Jay (1974). *Compulsive gamblers.* New York: Harper and Row.

Lofland, John. (1971). *Analyzing social settings.* Belmont, CA: Wadsworth.

Lofland, John, and Lofland, Lyn. (1984). *Analyzing social settings: A guide to qualitative observation and analysis* (2nd ed.). Belmont, CA: Wadsworth.

Martineau, Harriet. (1838/1989). *How to observe morals and manners.* London: Chad Knight. New Brunswick, NJ: Transaction.

Middleman, Lou. (1987). *Writing across the curriculum workshop.* Virginia Polytechnic Institute and State University.

Miller, Eleanor. (1986). *Street woman.* Philadelphia: Temple University Press.

Myers, James. (1994). Nonmainstream body modification: Genital piercing, branding, burning, and cutting. In Patricia Adler and Peter Adler (Eds.), *Constructions of deviance: Social power, context, and interaction* (pp. 414–446). Belmont, CA: Wadsworth.

Nader, L. (1970). From anguish to exultation. In P. Golde (Ed.), *Women in the field* (pp. 97–116). Chicago: Aldine.

Neuman, W. Lawrence. (1991). *Social research methods: Qualitative and quantitative approaches.* Boston: Allyn and Bacon.

Nichols, John. (1974). *The Milagro beanfield war.* New York: Ballantine Books.

Oakley, A. (1981). Interviewing women: A contradiction in terms. In H. Roberts (Ed.), *Doing feminist research,* (pp. 30–61). London: Routledge & Kegan Paul.

Parkhill, Thomas. (1993). What's taking place: Neighborhood *Ramlilas* in Banaras. In Bradley R. Hertel and Cynthia Ann Humes (Eds.), *Living Banaras: Hindu Religion in cultural context* (pp. 103–126). Albany: State University of New York Press.

Piliavin, Irving, Rodin, Judith, and Piliavin, Jan Allyn. (1969). Good Samaritanism: An underground phenomenon? *Journal of Personality and Social Psychology, 13,* 289–299.

Powdermaker, Hortense. (1966). *Stranger and friend: The way of an anthropologist.* New York: W. W. Norton and Co.

Prus, Robert, and Irini, Styllianoss. (1988). *Hookers, rounders, and desk clerks: The social organization of the hotel community.* Salem, WI: Sheffield.

Punch, Maurice. (1986). *The politics and ethics of fieldwork.* Beverly Hills: Sage.

Punch, Maurice. (1994). Politics and ethics in qualitative research. In Norman K. Denzin and Yvonna S. Lincoln (Eds.), *Handbook of qualitative research* (pp. 83–98). Thousand Oaks, CA: Sage.

Richardson, Laurel. (1994). Writing: A method of inquiry. In Norman K. Denzin and Yvonna S. Lincoln (Eds.), *Handbook of qualitative research* (pp. 516–529). Thousand Oaks, CA: Sage.

Roadburg, Allan. (1980). Breaking relationships with research subjects: Some problems and suggestions. In William B. Shaffir, Robert A. Stebbins, and Allan Turowetz (Eds.), *Fieldwork experience: Qualitative approaches to social research* (pp. 281–291). New York: St. Martin's Press.

Rosecrance, John. (1990). You can't tell the players without a scorecard: A typology of horse players. In Clifton D. Bryant (Ed.), *Deviant behavior: Readings in the sociology of norm violations* (pp. 348–370). New York: Hemisphere.

Rousseau, A. M. (1981). *Shopping bag ladies: Homeless women speak about their lives.* New York: Pilgrim Press.

Russell, Betty. (1991). *Silent sisters: A study of homeless women.* New York: Hemisphere.

Sagarin, E., and Moneymaker, J. (1979). The dilemma of researcher immunity. In C. B. Klockars and F. W. O'Connor (Eds.), *Deviance and decency* (pp. 175–193). Beverly Hills: Sage.

Shaffir, William B., and Strebbins, Robert A. (Eds.). (1991). *Experiencing fieldwork: An inside view of qualitative research.* Newbury Park, CA: Sage.

Shaffir, William B., Strebbins, Robert A., and Allan Turowetz, Allan. (Eds.). (1980). *Fieldwork experience: Qualitative approaches to social research.* New York: St. Martin's Press.

Sieber, Joan. (1982). *The ethics of social research: Fieldwork, regulation, and publication.* New York: Springer-Verlag.

Spradley, James P. (1970). *You owe yourself a drunk: An ethnography of urban nomads.* Boston: Little, Brown.

Spradley, James P., and McCurdy, D. W. (1975). *The cultural experience: Ethnography in complex society.* Palo Alto, CA: Science Research Associates.

Stacey, Judith. (1991). *Brave new families: Stories of domestic upheaval in late twentieth century America.* New York: Basic Books.

Stombler, Mindy, and Martin, Patricia Yancey. (1994). Bringing women in, keeping women down: Fraternity "little sister" organizations. *Journal of Contemporary Ethnography, 23,* 150–184.

Thompson, Hunter S. (1979). *Gonzo papers: Vol. 1. The great shark hunt.* New York: Fawcett Popular Library.

Tuchman, Barbara. (1989, Feb. 2). Historical winner of two Pulitzer Prizes dies at age 77. *New York Times.*

Ueland, B. (1938). *If you want to write: A book about art, independence and spirit.* Saint Paul, MN: Graywolf.

van den Berghe, P. (1968). Research in South Africa. In G. Sjoberg (Ed.), *Ethics, politics and social research* (pp. 183–197). Cambridge, MA: Schenkman.

Van Maanen, John. (1982). Fieldwork on the beat: This being an account of the manners and customs of an ethnographer in an American police department. In John Van Maanen, James M. Dabbs, Jr., and Robert R. Faulkner (Eds.), *Varieties of qualitative research* (pp. 103–151). Beverly Hills: Sage.

Van Maanen, John. (1988). *Tales of the field: On writing ethnography.* Chicago: University of Chicago Press.

Wallace, Walter. (1971). *The logic of science in sociology.* Chicago: Aldine.

Wallis, R. (1977). The moral career of a research sociologist. In C. Bell and H. Newby (Eds.), *Doing Sociological Research* (pp. 149–169). London: Allen & Unwin.

Warren, Carol A. B. (1982). *The court of last resort: Mental illness and the law.* Chicago: University of Chicago Press.

Warren, Carol A. B. (1988). *Gender issues in field research.* Newbury Park, CA: Sage.

Wax, Rosalie. (1971). *Doing fieldwork: Warnings and advice.* Chicago: The University of Chicago Press.

Wax, Rosalie. (1979). Gender and age in fieldwork and fieldwork education: No good think is done by any man alone *Social Problems, 26,* 509–522.

Weiner, L. (1984). Sisters of the road. In E. H. Monkkonen (Ed.), *Walking to work: Tramps in America 1790–1985* (pp. 171–188). Lincoln: University of Nebraska Press.

Whyte, William Foote. (1955). *Street corner society: The social structure of an Italian slum* (2nd ed.). Chicago: University of Chicago Press.

Wodehouse, P. G. (1976). *Jeeves, Jeeves, Jeeves.* New York: Avon Books.

Wolf, Margery. (1992). *A thrice-told tale: Feminism, postmodernism, and ethnographic responsibility.* Stanford, CA: Stanford University Press.

Wolfgang, Marvin. (1976). Ethical issues of research in criminology. In P. Nejelski (Ed.), *Social research in conflict with law and ethics* (pp. 25–34). Cambridge, MA: Ballinger.

Glossary/Index